A Handful of Ashes

For my children,
Steven, Rebecca, Megan & Regan.

Always remember you can achieve the impossible, because you have experienced the unimaginable. The hardest part is not losing someone we love, but the lifetime it will take learning to live without them.

I have experienced grief many times throughout my life and I had always believed myself to have been left truly heartbroken by the aftermath of a death. It's only my opinion, but I think the word 'heartbroken' is used far too casually. It is associated with pretty much anything that instigates a sudden or unexpected onset of sadness. Should losing a job, a cancelled holiday, a teenage relationship breaking up or even the most acrimonious divorce, really categorise someone as being left completely heartbroken? It seems that more frequently than not, it does. I expect there are many who would argue this point with me, feeling that they have had their hearts broken, but I still doubt they truly have. I believe that real heartbreak can only be felt following the death and separation from someone you love unconditionally and unimaginably deep. The difference in the levels of depth that this one emotion can reach cannot be explained in words. It truly is the worst kind of mental and physical suffering anyone will ever experience.

Growing from a young child into a teenager, I grieved on many occasions for the loss of adored pets, slowly beginning to realise the change in the magnitude of my grief, depending on my attachment and love for them. Unfortunately, and by the time I had reached my early twenties, the loss of animals had played no part whatsoever in preparing me for when my grand-parents died, all within the space of seventeen months of each other. I was sure that the grief I had endured through losing these very close family members had reached its ultimate peak, but I was wrong. In April 1998, my Dad became unwell and was quickly diagnosed with bowel cancer. He underwent an operation to remove the tumour but afterwards, he was told that the cancer had spread to his liver. I never contemplated for one moment that my Dad would die. He was such a fighter and despite being my Dad, he was also my hero, so if anyone could beat cancer, he would. But sadly he couldn't and on 21st December 1998, he passed away aged 62 and I was left totally destroyed.

I have spent over twenty years living a life without my Dad. As a family we always spoke about him and I know that this became a huge strength to me and helped me over the years to keep him close. Frequently reminiscing and sharing our memories of him and all the funny stories of his 'Granddad antics' kept my Dad in our conversations and always at the forefront of our minds. This enabled us to carry on rebuilding our own lives without him physically being part of them anymore.

To lose a parent is beyond devastating, something you don't want to imagine and you can't begin to comprehend it. Time progresses, you get older and realize that we are all heading in the same direction and therefore, death is inevitable. Gone are those moments when you thought that maybe you and your family, in some miraculous way, will live forever and elude the circle of life. Death is a natural certainty of life, but that doesn't make it any easier to accept when it turns up uninvited at your door and takes a loved one. I never imagined that any grief would feel worse or destroy me more than that of losing my Dad, but my God, how wrong was I?

My son died. It's hard to write that. I look at those three little words over and over and I still find them shocking and unbelievable. Danny was just 25 years and 6 days old when he died in his sleep. There was no illness, no accident, no suicide, no warning or reason, he just fell asleep and never woke up. I had been blessed with the most amazing family, three gorgeous sons and two beautiful daughters, Dan being the second eldest of my five perfectly healthy and beautiful children.
Nothing, not even losing my Dad, came close or had resemblance in preparing me for the magnitude of this unimaginable and excruciating pain that instantly engulfed me upon finding my beautiful child lifeless and cold.

My family has been obliterated by Danny's death. It wasn't normal and it certainly wasn't the timeline of life. I drifted through the days that followed his death and began to realise that the person I was, the mum, the wife, the daughter, the sister and friend, everything that had made me who I was, had also died with Danny. The destruction of so many lives had happened in that instant of me opening his bedroom door; I just never realized it at the time. Alongside the constant physical pain caused by the sudden separation from losing my son, I couldn't cope with the grief of losing myself. I couldn't function or breathe properly. I couldn't think logically or stop crying for any consistent amount of time to even consider my other children. Everything had been smashed to smithereens and no amount of 'give it time' or 'coming to terms' will ever make any parent accept the loss of a healthy child, or help siblings accept the loss of a brother at such a young age and certainly not in these circumstances.

The perfect, beautiful and happy family life we had all shared was now permanently destroyed and we would never be complete again. Part of us all had died with Danny. An irreplaceable piece of what held us so tightly together, not just as a family, but more of who we were as individuals, was suddenly gone and it was never coming back. My child had just fallen asleep and died, leaving the rest of us to deal with every raw feeling and turbulent emotion that real heartbreak brings with it and facing the most painful of all journeys imaginable, a life and future without Danny.

This is my story.

Daniel Jay

Daniel Jay Brown was born on Tuesday 3rd March 1992 at 10.35pm. Spontaneous from the start, he made a speedy entrance into this world arriving ten days early. I had an inkling that my second baby boy was going to be unique as I had suffered with morning sickness practically every day from the first, to the last of my 38 weeks and 4 day pregnancy. Unlike his bigger brother Steven, who was 13 months older and had slept 8 hours through the night from birth, Danny immediately showed signs of being the complete opposite! He wanted feeding every four hours during the day and thoroughly enjoyed a little 'top up' every four hours during the night. He would start having a little moan about 10 minutes beforehand, giving me just enough time to spring into action!

That most precious auburn haired, whirlwind of a little boy grew so quickly from the funniest, mischievously impish and cheekiest child, into your typical party going, adventure and thrill seeking teenager, finally maturing into the kindest, most selfless and loving adult you could ever have the pleasure to know. You truly didn't have to spend very long in Dan's company to really get to know him well. Whether you had been fortunate to have had a five minute chat or shared a ten year friendship with him, what you saw was exactly what you got, there were definitely no grey areas with him. Danny was certainly no fool, in fact he was very clued up on almost everything. I can honestly say, there were definitely no flies on our Dan! He wore his heart on his sleeve, was extremely quick witted and had an endearing cheeky charm about him. Always referred to by others as a genuine and fun loving young man who, and I know it sounds cliché, really did have the ability to light up a room. He had a natural gift of being able to strike up conversation with anyone, from any walk of life about absolutely anything! Having this unique gift to attract attention, people just liked being around him because of his warm nature, boundless energy and an infectious laugh and personality. Danny also had an endless variety of thought provoked facial expressions. Believe me, that boy really could say more with his classic, silent facial movements than any amount of spoken words ever could! He did enjoy an occasional good moan, but the majority of the time he was smiling and when he did, the bonus of having perfect teeth only enhanced that most beautiful smile and his whole face would beam!

Those of us who are blessed to be Danny's immediate family and of course those who were privileged to have been part of his very large group of friends, will understand completely when I say that Danny never did anything in half measures. He was the most spontaneous and impulsive person ever. We had a comical conversation about this when I had once remarked that I didn't think anyone could be more spontaneous than I was, though I had come to believe that Dan really could give me a run for my money! In response to this, he closed his eyes, raised his eyebrows and with half a smile and a little nod of his head, he silently confirmed that he already knew he did! From a very young child, Danny always had to be the first to do something. He absolutely loved seeing others react to his 'element of surprise' and was truly born to organise. Although saying that, during times of making any kind of social plan for him and his friends, he'd constantly moan about their lack of motivation or input enthusiasm! It's fair to say his friends had firmly placed him in the centre of everything they did and were more than happy to follow his lead. He liked it that way, often laughing as he enjoyed referring to himself as "Always the shepherd, never a sheep". He was the most sociable and happy-go-lucky type, but by no means overly extrovert. He just had something about him which would draw people towards him. He was intelligent and fun to be around and I always saw him as a, 'Why be like the rest of the crowd, when you can stand out in the crowd' type of person.

One of Danny's most exclusive qualities was his view and attitude to life and not forgetting his astounding uniqueness, in constantly having some kind of drama following him around like the air he breathed! There was always something unbelievable happening either to, or around him. Rarely did he come home without having a new story to tell, which of course would usually amount to him either laughing hysterically whilst trying to explain or whinging about it at great lengths. He also had the most incredible luck, which he developed into a real talent whilst working as a cashier for William Hill bookmakers. Obviously he couldn't gamble within that specific organisation, but that didn't bother him, because Dan had an online account with Betfred! He would always share his knowledge and any punter tips with his friends and family and would encourage all of us old enough, to open a betting account with one bookie or another, so we could qualify for a specific 'sign up deal' or free bet! He frequently turned the most minimal amount of money into an astonishing megabucks win!! He valued the opinion of others, was good a listener and gave very good advice. Danny was naturally kind natured and would always be the first to offer his compassionate shoulder to cry on. He had the patience of a saint when helping his younger siblings, Megan and Regan with their homework, but he certainly wouldn't let himself be taken for granted and nor would he tolerate the company of someone if he felt they weren't pulling their weight! His sarcasm to trivialities could render you speechless and he never held a grudge. He didn't have any kind of temper as such, perhaps a rarely used bark more than any kind of bite. He was definitely never in the wrong and nothing was ever his fault!

Dan just loved life, living each day to the full and literally making every second count. He made plans, fulfilled many dreams, always strived to be the best at what he enjoyed and would be more than happy to go that extra mile when necessary. Danny was reliable and dependable and always there when you needed someone to fight your corner and have your back. He was compassionate and had wisdom well beyond his years, he would be brutally honest and completely loyal to those he loved and was always there to lean on for support.

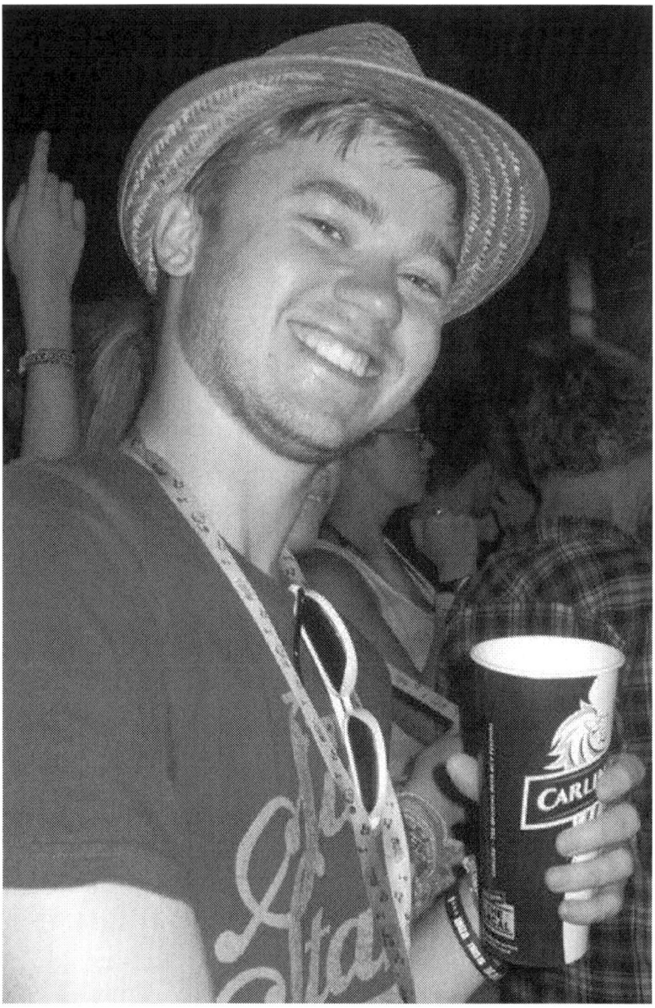

Australia

In the summer of 2013, Danny quit his job and set off to spend a year in Australia. He flew out on his own to meet up with a couple of friends who had travelled out a few months earlier. He hit the ground running when he arrived in Sydney and enjoyed living a little too long like he was on a permanent holiday and with a few grand in his bank account, money was in abundance! He stayed in regular contact; usually face timing us as he happily staggered home from a bar in the early hours of the morning, or from his bedsit nursing a slight hangover in the afternoon! Within the first couple of months, he came close to running out of money. He couldn't find regular work and things were beginning to get a bit desperate. He phoned to ask if we would be able to get him a flight home if no job came about in the next couple weeks, which obviously I said we would if things got that dire. He was struggling with his rent and food and felt it wasn't turning out to be the experience he had hoped for. However, Dan being Dan, his perseverance literally paid off after advertising his skills and availability to do practically anything that was listed on Gumtree! One strange chap emailed to ask if Dan would go to his house for a massage ... Thankfully, things weren't that desperate, so he didn't respond to that one!

He finally secured some labouring work with the other lads, and eventually started earning a good wage. Although work came in fits and starts, he really managed his money well. He became a Jack of all Trades whilst he was there. He painted houses and fences and even turned his hand to doing some landscape gardening. He messaged me on one occasion to tell me he was "in prison". I can't tell you how frantic I was, until he messaged back with 'Hahaha' and smiley Emoji faces, to say that he had started working in a newly built correctional facility, painting and fitting out the cells and bathrooms! Now he could pay his rent and was eating fewer takeaways. He began saving some money and finally started to enjoy his Australian adventure. He would always message or face time us every few days, usually at some obscure time! I didn't care; I just loved hearing from him and what he was up to. I would wait with anticipation for an update on his whereabouts and goings on and there was always an excitement overload seeing pictures being uploaded while reading his text messages. One morning he sent me some photos of 'something weird' that had come up on his leg and asked if I thought he should get it looked at. I Googled these images and upon comparison, thought it looked like a spider bite. I asked him if it was and he said 'No Mum, definitely not', to which I started to panic because it really did look like a typical spider bite, but as he said it wasn't, my unprofessional opinion told me that the only other option was that it must be a tick! I visualised this being so much worse than any spider, obviously this had clearly buried itself into his skin and was now going to give him Lyme disease! I told him to get straight down to the hospital and get it looked at! Thankfully and being a good boy, he did exactly that d after a couple of hours and some treatment, he was packed off back to the bedsit with a course of antibiotics. After a few days, the infection subsided and the swelling went down leaving his leg looking nearly normal again. However, it wasn't until he came home that he told me that it was a spider bite, information he had shared with his sister Becky but hadn't wanted me to know and worry at the time!

The months flew by for us at home as Danny continued to meander his way from Sydney to Cairns via the Gold Coast and then up to Darwin, onto Broome and then down to Perth. He made so many friends, created so many memories and achieved so many 'once in a lifetime' experiences. He went down to Melbourne and watched England v Australia play for the Ashes. He hand fed kangaroos, swam with turtles and snorkelled at the Great Barrier Reef, he travelled into and around the Blue Mountains, travelled to the Rain Forest and enjoyed swimming at the waterfalls in Josephine Falls. He camped on Frazer Island and told me he had never seen so many stars in the sky as he did there, he enjoyed kayaking with wild dolphins and did a sky dive over Byron Bay just after sunrise. All too soon for Danny, his time down-under was over and without mentioning it, he flew back to the UK in June 2014.

Danny wanted his home-coming to be a surprise and late in the afternoon of 23rd June, there on the doorstep stood the familiar figure of my son. I was practically hysterical seeing him walk in. I jumped up and swung my arms around his neck and hugged him so tight, just not wanting to let go of him and completely unaware of everyone else standing there who were waiting to welcome him home. I couldn't believe he was home; it was just so good to finally have him back. My family reunited, perfectly complete and all of us together under the one roof again. We all sat in the lounge chatting, Dan getting a detailed analysis of what had been happening at home and us hearing all that he had done while he had been away but hadn't mentioned when messaging or face timing. I remember I just sat there staring at him and holding onto his arm, just in case he had the urge to jump up and go elsewhere! Listening to him talk all about what he'd done during the past year was beyond amazing. My boy had finally come home and although it was Dan sitting next to me, there was something different about him. He was very jet-lagged, but he was calmer and more content than when he had left us twelve months before. He was now sporting a bit of a beard and his body had thickened out slightly. He looked manlier, more mature. My God, I really had missed him so much and although I had not witnessed the transition, it was clear to see that Danny had grown from a young lad into a man. He had developed an independence and responsibility whilst he had been away and had changed from 'one of the lads' into this beautiful adult that now sat beside me. I guess when your children are with you day in day out, you never notice the caterpillar to butterfly moment, but he had been gone for twelve months and the difference in him was visible for all to see. Danny had thoroughly enjoyed each and every life changing experiences that Australia had offered him. He was happy to be home, but said there was just so much to see and do there that he had made a promise to himself that one day, he would definitely go back.

Luckily for Danny and within two weeks from arriving home and through a friend of a friend, he'd secured an engineer apprenticeship with an access control security firm in London. They offered excellent career prospects once he was fully qualified, and in the meantime paid him a decent wage which put money in his pocket whilst he was learning. Along with a company car thrown in as part of the package, it wasn't long before Dan was driving up and down the country for work purposes. One of the first things he did was to renew his West Ham season ticket, it was then time once again to get back out and be part of enjoying the many social gatherings with his large group of friends. Dan's life was going from strength to strength and just a few months later in February 2015, on a boy's weekend up in Liverpool and whilst waiting for a taxi outside 'Popworld', he met and fell head over heels in love with the most beautiful girl called Meg.

Life was perfect and Danny was ecstatically happy.

March 2017

March kicked off with Danny celebrating his 25th birthday with family and friends. Meg came down from Liverpool on Wednesday 1st March and took Dan up London for a meal on 'The Yacht', a floating restaurant moored at Embankment, on the Thursday. Friday the 3rd of March was Dan's birthday, so we all went out to the local Mexican restaurant and sat there for a few hours just chatting, laughing, eating and drinking. It was the most perfect evening and a fabulous way to end his 25th birthday. It was also the first time ever that all ten of us had ever been out together, Rich and me, Megan, Regan and Steve, Danny and Becky with their partners. I was sitting opposite Dan and vividly remember looking along at my beautiful kids and thinking how perfect it all was and how complete and tight we were as a family. On the Saturday Dan had a party round at his Dad's house with his friends, he came rolling in just before 3am, slightly worse for wear and unsuccessfully trying to be quiet whilst making a drink and playing with Luna, before heading down to his room! On the Sunday he took Meg off to Harry Potter World, this was something he had bought her for Christmas, but it had originally coincided with the gift of a trip to Poland, so he had rescheduled it for the 5th. I was at work and messaged him to ask how the party had gone and how he was feeling, to which he replied, "I'm OK, not really hung-over as such, just a bit tired". I knew that was one of the most under-exaggerations of the truth I had ever heard!

It had been the busiest of weekends for Dan and he was the happiest I had ever seen him, his life was absolutely perfect. Steve and Dan had also been busy for a good few weeks, planning and booking fights and accommodation for a three week holiday travelling from west to east coast America, that they and their girlfriends were going on in June. It had originally started as a short break to attend the wedding of a distant cousin on their Dad's side of the family. However, what with Dan's ridiculously, spontaneous enthusiasm and Steven's happy go lucky encouragement, the pair of them decided to build an amazing holiday around this event. Their finalised arrangements had them all flying to LA, visiting San Francisco, onto Las Vegas, across to Ohio, up to Niagara Falls, down to New York and squeezing in the wedding in Rhode Island, before Steve and Nicole flew home, leaving Danny and Meg to travel onto Washington before they too flew home a few days later. Dan was also in the middle of organising his best mate's stag do, as a group of sixteen of them were off to Bucharest for a few days. Danny had been asked to be a best man at the forthcoming wedding of two of his closest friends from school who had been in a relationship since they were 14 and were now finally getting hitched!

On the Monday morning Dan returned to work after dropping Meg off at Euston station, as she was heading back to Liverpool. He phoned me after she had left to tell me that she had 'got off OK' and although it was a bit of a rush, he'd seen her onto the train and given her a kiss before he had to rush off. He would always give me an update on how she was when she went back and was happy to say that she wasn't quite as upset as usual, because it was only four days until Friday and she'd be back, this time with her Mum and step Dad, to celebrate my 50th birthday on Saturday 11th.

On Wednesday March 8th 2017, Danny walked in from work just after 4pm. He was his usual bright and happy self and we had a chat about what our day had been like. He told me how he had dropped Becky off at the station on his way to work and said he'd had a 'nightmare journey' getting there because the traffic was a joke. We stood on the patio and continued chatting about how I wanted to have lots of family photos taken on Saturday at the party as we would all be dressed up smart. I had bought a large photobox cardboard frame for us all to stand behind, Danny started laughing and said 'Mum, the seven of us will never all fit behind that', I said we would, but if he was right, we would work something out as long as I had loads of updated photos of my gorgeous babies. With our conversation over, I watched him walk down the garden to his room; he had his work bag slung over his shoulder, his head was down and he was busy texting on his phone. He appeared at the back door some ten minutes later with his gym kit and said he was meeting his friend Mike, because they were "in training" to do the Nuclear Rush race in May.

Danny's idea of training was treadmill and sauna, usually followed by a 'Cheeky Nandos', but as he breezed out of the door, he called out to say that he'd be back for dinner in about an hour or so. He returned home just before 6pm and took his German shepherd dog Luna for a walk. He came in complaining about how she wouldn't walk and had been a nightmare and that he had practically dragged her around the block! I laughed and made a comment to him as I passed him in the hall, patting him on the shoulder as I made my way upstairs. He continued manoeuvring Luna through the house and towards the garden before going into the kitchen to make his dinner of chicken and rice. After I came back downstairs, I went straight into the lounge and sat with Megan and Becky and watched TV. Dan and Rich ate their dinner together in the dining room and I occasionally heard Dan laughing at the You Tube videos Regan was showing him. I heard them using the printer but didn't realise they were printing off details for a surprise trip that Richard had booked to take me to Italy, a few weeks after my birthday. Just before 8pm and with a "See you later", Danny wandered off down the garden to his room to watch the Barcelona football match.

Thursday March 9th

I woke Megan and Regan up for school at the usual time of 7.30am. We came downstairs and sat up the table having breakfast. It was a lovely sunny day and I let the cats out and watched one make a dash to the tree outside Danny's cabin, which had Robins nesting in it. In slippers and dressing gown I walked down the garden towards the tree to chase the cat away and she ran into the neighbour's garden and I returned to the house. Within half hour, Megan had left for school and Regan would usually have set off not long after her to meet his friend, leaving me in peace to start tidying up and ushering Danny and Becky off to work. This particular morning however, Regan was taking part in an event for his school at a local sports centre, so we left the house together shortly after 8.30am. This finished just before midday and after dropping Regan at school, I drove home and pulled up outside the house at 12.10pm.

I saw Danny's car was still parked outside and my first thought was that he must have travelled up to London for work by train. I walked in to find Becky in the kitchen making her lunch as she was just getting ready to leave for work. I asked her if Danny had gone on the train as his car was still outside. She responded with, 'I haven't seen Danny this morning; I thought he had left before I got up'. Thinking this was unusual and looking through the window down the garden at his cabin, I could see the blinds were still pulled down. I opened the patio door and started walking towards his room and suddenly became aware that I hadn't received any texts from him that morning. I was nearly halfway down the garden when I broke into a run. It took me less than ten seconds to get from the house to his room and I momentarily paused outside on the step, listening for some kind of sound or movement from the inside before I knocked on the door. Danny always locked himself in his room when he went to bed, but I felt reassured that he was up because it was unlocked as the handle moved freely as I turned it. Opening his door and lifting the blind, I looked into his room.

The only thing I was aware of at the time was the silence in the room and the stillness of Danny lying so peacefully on his bed. I stood in the doorway for a few seconds just looking at him, believing he was asleep, but that he had just not heard me enter the room. It's strange how every single detail is heightened when you are suddenly faced with a situation that you have never been in before. Dan was wearing a grey t shirt with New York Yankees written across the front of it in blue, and pair of grey converse tracksuit bottom. I immediately recognised these items as being the same as he had worn home from the gym, the night before. His head was resting on his pillow, but was slightly turned to the left, so from where I was standing I couldn't fully see his face. His left foot was on the bed, but his right was casually hanging over the side. He had no socks on. His feet were so pale. My gaze was then drawn to his hands, which were comfortably resting upon his chest. It was the positioning of his fingers, which looked so un-natural, that for the briefest of moments I couldn't actually understand what was wrong with my beautiful boy. He was so still and the room was deathly silent. In those first few seconds, I guess I must have been trying to absorb the reality of what I was seeing, yet at the same time wasn't quite sure exactly what that was. I remember very softly saying his name, as I stepped into the room and slowly walked towards him, not taking my eyes off of him until I was beside him and could now clearly see his sleeping face. I gently placed my hand on his right arm but he didn't respond, I glanced at his chest and realised he wasn't breathing, he was cold and his eyes remained closed, my beautiful Danny had died.

Instantly, that feeling of cautious uncertainty was brutally replaced with the most overwhelming and horrifically gut-wrenching realisation that my precious child was dead. I started screaming, pleading, shaking and begging him to wake up. At that precise moment, really believing that if I screamed loud enough, I could stop everything that was happening and Danny would hear me and open his beautiful dark brown eyes. But he couldn't hear me and he didn't open his eyes because he was gone, he'd been gone for hours and had laid there all alone, while the rest of us had just carried on with our day and lives as normal. Danny had come into this world in a light and bright room, filled with nurses, noise and love but had left it in a dark silent one, all alone, with no one by his side. The pain and guilt I constantly feel because of this is totally indescribable and something I know, I will never come to terms with. I had always believed that I would have some kind of sixth sense in knowing if there was something wrong with any one of my five children, if I wasn't with them at the time. I had walked down the garden earlier that morning and had stood less than ten feet from him and hadn't had any kind of feeling that something so terrible had happened. For the rest of my life, I will live with the heartache of not knowing if he had felt unwell and called out for help, or if given the chance, I could have saved him, if only I had opened his door at 7.30am. But I didn't know and now I was too late to help him, because he was gone forever.

It truly is impossible to imagine what it is like to walk into the bedroom of a perfectly fit and healthy 25 year old and find them dead. There had been no sign or warning that something was wrong with Dan. He wasn't unwell and hadn't had an accident; there was nothing, just silence and stillness. Finding Danny like this made no sense at all and I completely lost control. Suddenly everything that seconds before was moving in slow motion, was now beyond frantic and totally chaotic. How had my beautiful son gone down to his room to watch the football, settled down on his bed, fallen asleep and died? I was now on the floor, kneeling beside him and looking around his room for the cause, a reason or explanation of how or why he was laying here lifeless. My head was racing, maybe he had accidentally electrocuted himself, hit his head or choked and even for a split second I stupidly considered that he had taken his own life. But there was nothing. Hearing my screams, Becky came running down the garden. She had assumed that Danny was unwell or hurt but realised it was more serious when she approached his cabin and heard me saying, "Oh my darling, what have you done". I turned to see my beautiful daughter standing at the door with her hands up at her face as I screamed at her, "He's dead". She started crying and screaming as she ran back to the house to get her phone. Within seconds, she came back into his room and said "we need to get him onto the floor; we need to do CPR,

Mum". It wasn't physically possible for us to move Danny on to the floor and I said "we are too late baby, he's gone". She had the most devastated look on her face as she cried, "No Mum please, I need to try". I just nodded. It was such a surreal, hopeless and desperate situation. Dan had been gone for hours and all I could think of was that Becky would feel like she had failed or let him down or feel responsible for not being able to bring him back. Watching my daughter frantically trying to revive her brother was heartbreaking, because I truly believe that she knew he was gone, but she was not about to give up on him, she wanted more than anything to help him and didn't know what else to do. It was the only act of true devoted love she could do for him, even though it was devastatingly obvious to us that we were both far too late to save him.

Within minutes, two ambulances and a rapid response vehicle pulled up outside and our home. Five paramedics ran into the house and asked me where he was, I just pointed down the garden to his room, they continued running and carrying every piece of life-saving equipment they had with them, but upon reaching Danny, they instantly knew that it was far too late to do anything and despite my pleading and begging for them to help, they pronounced his time of death at 12.31 pm.

It had taken just 21 minutes for my life to go from perfectly beautiful and normal, to being decimated beyond recognition forever. Now standing in the middle of the garden, the silence was broken as Becky said, "Mum, I need to ring Dad". Those few words were like being hit in the chest with a sledgehammer. This was really happening to us, I felt physically sick knowing that this was real and that we were never going to wake up from this nightmare. It was real and now we had to make it real for everyone else by phoning them and telling them that Danny had died. I didn't know how to make that sort of phone call. How do you tell your family, his siblings, his girlfriend, his mates and work colleagues that he has just died? It was too horrifically shocking. This just doesn't happen. The lives of young fit and healthy people don't just end because they have fallen asleep. He had only turned 25 six days before. I didn't know how to say those awful words and I wouldn't be able to give them a reason or explanation to the same question when they asked me 'How'? There is no way you can soften the blow or gently break such tragically unexpected news like this to those you love, when you are making a call. I was in such shock and disbelief myself that I just felt I wasn't mentally ready, let alone emotionally stable enough to control how I would actually say it. But the clock kept ticking and taking me further away from finding him, so feeling totally destroyed, I realised I had to start making those impossible calls. I was numb and went into some sort of auto pilot mode. I really don't remember how many or even who I called, let alone what I told them or whether I explained the very little I knew of what had happened to Danny, other than that he had died.

I can though, vividly recall every brutal detail of the first two calls that I made on that day. The first was to Steven and the second to Richard. Honestly, both of their heartbroken screams will echo in my head for the rest of my life.

I wouldn't leave Danny alone in his room, so I lay down beside him and gently stroked his beautiful face and thick auburn hair. I knew that I needed to stay with him now for as long as I possibly could and make every passing second so very precious. I just stared at him, kissing his cheek and taking in every single millimetre and detail of his beautiful sleeping face. I noticed a few tiny scars on him that I hadn't noticed in years. One was on the right-hand side of his cheek, in the 'smile' crease just above his lip. This had occurred when he was about 3 years old and was running through the lounge and had fallen head first into a box of Lego. This accident required a trip to the hospital for the little wound to be glued back together. There were also a couple of small chicken pox scars, one on his forehead and another just beside his eye. Steve, Danny and Becky had all caught chicken pox at around the same time, but yet again, Dan being Dan got it first and was a whole lot worse and had suffered with more spots than the other two put together. And here they were, these tiny little marks unnoticed for so many years but still clearly visible on him. Proof of just some injuries and illnesses he had endured and I had nursed him through from childhood. Their cause forgotten until now, yet nevertheless they had remained forever evident on the adult bearded face of my precious 25 years and 6 day old son.

People kept coming into his room and asking questions, what had he done the night before? Was he taking any medication? Had he been unwell? They were trying to unlock his phone and were looking in his gym bag. Everything was a blur but also vividly real at the same time. I suddenly found myself sitting up the dining table with his passport and driving licence in my hands and giving a statement to the paramedic. "Full name and date of birth of the deceased" she said. I felt like I had been punched in the face. This was my Danny they were talking about. I didn't want his name being written on some standard form alongside the word 'Deceased'. I stood up and said, "I can't do this, I am going back to be with Dan". She responded with "I'm afraid you can't be down there now until the police arrive". I must have shot her such glare as I said, "I don't give a shit this is my home and I was with him before any of you arrived and I am not leaving him in there on his own". Another paramedic quickly adding, "its fine, of course you must be with him and I'll come with you if that's ok?'. I nodded and we both left the dining room and walked down the garden in silence to Danny's cabin.

One of the most painful things of that day was being so aware that the time I was now spending with him was running out. It really is like being a grain of sand in an hour glass. I knew the police were on their way and that the coroner had been called. All these people would eventually arrive and they would take him away and that would be it, he would be gone from us and his home forever. I would never have this time with him again, being able to look at him, hold him, lay beside him and rest my head on his chest. I just wanted to be with him and keep him here in his home for as long as was possible. There was a lot of muffled talking but I wasn't listening to anything that was being said until I became aware that it was only the paramedic, Danny and I who were in the room and that he was speaking to me. "He looks so peaceful, I know there is really nothing I can say to comfort you, but I believe he wouldn't have known anything about it. He's not in what we call a 'stressed position'. He would have felt no pain; he has just passed away peacefully in his sleep". He was right. I didn't take any comfort from it. The situation unfolding was just too shocking to take notice of anything that was happening or being said. I truly just wanted everything to stop, everyone to go away and leave me with Danny, laying there holding him and never letting him go. I kept thinking how many lives were now destroyed because of this. He had been ripped away from us so quickly that our perfect family unit was forever broken beyond repair. I visualised his beautiful Meg in Liverpool being told what had happened, their future life together suddenly obliterated in one short sentence and the finality of his presence within a circle of friends, many of whom had only spoken to him hours before.

I couldn't say for sure whether the time passed quickly or slowly up to the point when the two police officers eventually arrived, allowing the paramedics to leave. Family members that had rushed to our home and stood in silence in the garden and outside Dan's room for hours in total disbelief of what had happened had also left, leaving just one policewoman, my Mum, Rich and myself with Dan. Mum and Rich had gone up to the house some time before leaving me and the policewoman alone with Danny in his room. Nothing was said; I just laid beside him, cradling him the best I could, stroking his soft hair and face. I believe it was about 5.30pm when I heard footsteps on the gravel outside the cabin and looked up to see two dark suited men standing in the doorwayOver Five hours after finding Danny, the undertakers had arrived. It was the most sickeningly surreal sight. The empty numbness that had been with me for some time, drained away fast and was instantly replaced with one of desperate panic. This was it, this was the end. Less than 24 hours earlier we had both been standing in the garden, under the gazebo laughing and chatting about the party we were having here in two days time to celebrate my 50th birthday. I still had the image of him wandering through those same doors to grab his gym kit. Now two undertakers stood there and a black private ambulance was parked outside our home waiting to take Danny away. I watched as one of the undertakers clasped his hands, looked at me and began to say, "Please take all the time you need, I am so sorry for...." quickly standing up and interrupting him I said, "Don't you dare say that to me. Please, please don't say what you say to everyone else". He stopped in mid sentence, just nodded and squeezed my hand, turned and left the room with his colleague and the policewoman.

For the first time in hours just Dan and I were left alone, my last few moments ever with him in this room. Dan loved this room. This had been his private space for over ten years. He loved being down the garden and away from the house and had always enjoyed having an endless stream of mates coming round for game nights, movies, drinking and takeaways. Everything in there was his choice. He had bought himself a massive TV and had recently got himself a new bed, wardrobes and units. Dan loved any new gadget out, however big or small; he would be forever buying something off the internet because he had a use or need for it. There was always something turning up on the doorstep, so much so that I was on first name terms with the delivery driver from Amazon. Dan's PS4 and TV were wired up to a phenomenally deafening surround sound system; he had a projector and 80 inch retractable screen for movies. Anything that could be wirelessly connected in that room was, and his Amazon Alexa ensured he could listen to music as and when he wanted plus it turned his lights on and off without him having to move at all. Practically everything in his room he had chosen and bought for himself. He finally had it exactly how he wanted it and everything exactly where he wanted it to be. All the times I had spent in this room with him, helping him with decorating, cleaning and tidying, assembling new furniture or assisting him with moving it around. We had put up the blinds together, the pictures and mirrors. I had held the ladder whilst he had changed light bulbs, helped him position the security camera he had installed outside. There had been the countless occasions when we had searched together for misplaced school books, lost items of clothing, footwear, work uniform, his phone and his forever misplaced wallet. All the trips I had made down there in search of unreturned dinner plates and drinking glasses and always the weekly trip to empty his bin of discarded crisp packets and coke cans. None of this would now ever happen again. It all ended on this day. My arms had been the first to hold Danny when he came into this world and they were the last to ever hold him now he had left. His life was over and our lives with him in them had also come to an end. There was no more that I could do for him and although I didn't want too, I had to let him go. I wasn't sure what I was supposed to do now, as I stood alone in the middle of his room. I glanced over at his gym bag lying on the floor by the window, his trainers placed together by his door and his work jacket on the bean bag, all exactly where he had thrown it less than 24 hours ago. There was no more time; there were no more decisions to be made, no more options or choices left to take. The last grain of sand had dropped from my hour glass and all I could do now was just turn around, walk away and let someone else take care of him. I knelt down beside Dan one last time and kissed my precious boy on his forehead, whispering "I promise I will love you forever darling, I'll never let you go". I stood up and started to cry again and took one last look at the disbelieving sight of my beautiful child lying on his bed, before I left his room. The undertakers were outside and one escorted me up to the house and into the lounge. He closed the door behind me and that is where Danny's Dad, my Mum, Richard and I sat while it took those two dark suited strangers, less than five minutes to take our precious Danny out of his home forever.

I found myself standing up when I heard a trolley the other side of the closed door, crossing the wooden floor of the hall. Looking out of the window, I watched the brutal reality as those two undertakers wheeled the black cloth covered body of my son, down the path to the waiting private ambulance and routinely placed him into the back of it, before closing the doors and driving away.

Danny was gone and everything at that precise moment, completely stopped.

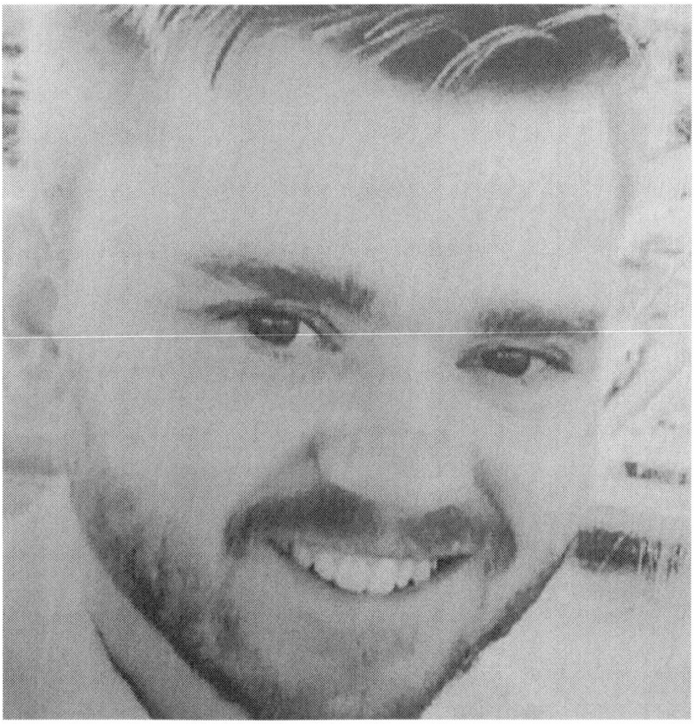

Broken Hearts & Hyacinths

I sat on the sofa, for what seemed like an endless period of time before Richard spoke, "Babe, shall I ring for Megan and Regan to come home?" The paramedic had contacted both of their schools just after 1pm, informing them of what had happened and that neither of them were to be told anything, other than I had been caught up and that a close friend would be picking them up from school. I nodded to Rich and he made that call. Within a few minutes and just before 6pm, the children arrived home. My Mum was sitting on the sofa opposite me and Rich, and got up to open the door as they walked up the path. I felt sick and started to shake and although the tears had not really stopped, suddenly they were streaming down my face. How on earth were we going to tell these two young, unsuspecting children that their fit and healthy 25 year old brother, who they were both laughing and joking with less than 24 hours ago, had suddenly died and gone from their lives forever? Megan walked into the lounge, immediately followed by Regan. They both stood side by side, but Megan was staring at me and instinctively said "What's wrong?"

I truly thought I was going to be sick, as I called them both over and sat them on the large poufee in front of me. "Something so very terrible has happened" I said. Neither of them moved a muscle as they sat there, they look so scared and confused and I just couldn't get anymore words out. I put my hands up to my face and said to Rich, "I can't say it". "Do you want me to?" he asked and I nodded. Their heads turned and they both looked directly at their Dad. I held their hands and closed my eyes as he took a deep breath and said, "Something terrible has happened, Danny has passed away and gone to heaven". They were silent for a couple of seconds until the reality of what had just been said hit them. Megan stood up and let out the most horrific noise and started screaming "NOT OUR DANNY, NO, NO, NO, Not our Danny?" Regan also started screaming and crying, but looked like he didn't understand that it was our Danny we were talking about. They were now both standing up and frantically thrashing about, it was as if they were trying to escape from under some invisible blanket of devastating reality that had just enshrouded them. We were now all crying hysterically and at the same time, I was desperately trying to catch hold of them, I managed to quickly pull both of them onto my lap and held them close and so very tight, hugging them as they gradually stopped screaming and completely broken hearted, they began to sob.

It was after 7pm when my Mum left with Megan and Regan as they had decided they wanted to spend the night at their Nan's. Dan's Meg, her Mum and Chris were driving down from Liverpool. I had managed to contact Meg's step Dad Chris, at work just after 1pm and inaudibly blurted out what had happened. I said I couldn't tell Meg over the phone and asked if he would tell Joanne (Meg's mum), and if she could tell Meg face to face. He said yes and that they would go and get Meg straightaway and immediately drive down to us, so I knew that they were well on their way. Richard and I hadn't eaten and we hardly spoke. We just sat in silence, totally lost and in shock. The hours were ticking away and I kept getting updates from Joanne as to where they were, but the traffic was atrocious and there seemed to be accidents dotted all the way from Liverpool to Essex and it was taking them hours to get anywhere. I couldn't sleep, even though physically, mentally and emotionally there was just nothing left inside me.

It was after 2am, and we were still waiting for Meg to arrive. They were now moving, but had been at a standstill on the motorway for hours. My heart was aching for them to get here as quickly as possible, but it had taken them so long to get anywhere. I could only imagine how awful it was for them all sitting in their car, for what had now been well over 12 hours, still being so far away and feeling so distraught. It had turned out to be the most horrendously long journey, only for them to eventually arrive and become a part of this tragic and unimaginable living nightmare. Rich was lying on the sofa in the lounge with his arms over his face and his eyes closed. I got up and came out into the dining room and just stared out of the back door at the garden and started to cry. The gazebo that had been standing there in preparation for the party was gone. It had been hurriedly taken down, allowing the undertakers to bring Danny up and through the house without any obstruction.

I looked down and Luna was sitting beside me. Upon finding Danny, she had come into his room whilst I was knelt beside him and had nudged his leg with her nose and I had shouted at her to get out. I'll never know if she sensed that something was wrong, but she immediately left his room and I had secured her behind a gate at the end of the garden, until after they had taken Dan away. I suddenly felt guilty; I hadn't given any thought to her all day. She looked up at me and tapped the glass of the door, her way of asking me to open it. She ran out onto the patio and stopped, looking back at me to join her. I stepped outside and opened the gate, giving her freedom to run down the garden, which she did as she made a dash for Danny's cabin and stopped when she reached his door. I walked down the garden and joined her on the step. The police had locked the cabin door and taken the key with them when the undertakers had left, saying that it had to be kept secure, until a cause of death had been established, as it was potentially a crime scene. I looked in though the window and noticed that the corner of the quilt, which Danny had pulled back before he had laid down, had been straightened out, leaving the bed looking normal and untouched. It was as if no one had been in there and as though nothing had happened in that room at all. His trainers, work boots and coat were still exactly where he had left them, but the room was dark and to me, it looked empty. And it hit me, that this was no longer his room anymore.

Danny had died in this room. My son had laid there for hours waiting for me to find him and now he was gone and the bed was neatly made, yet in my head, I could clearly see him as if he was still laying there. I had a flashback thought to when we put his newly purchased projector screen up, a few weeks previously. We had carried this big box down the garden and set it up precisely where he wanted it, on the top of two wardrobes, with his television unit in between them, allowing space for the screen to drop from ceiling to floor in front of the TV. He had stood on his bed, in full work gear with his security lanyard hanging around his neck; before turning on the wall mounted projector and watching the huge screen drop down. The happy and contented look he had on his face was absolutely priceless as he had pulled a cheeky half a smile and nodded his head before saying, "That looks the nuts, don't it Mum?" and it had, but now those moments, those facial expressions and conversations we had shared, were gone.

The events of this horrific day suddenly rushed into my head, along with a panic of where we would all go from here and that each and every day now and for the rest of my life, would just be another day without him. The garden was so still and peaceful, making it hard to accept that it had played centrepiece to such a tragic and chaotic event only 12 hours earlier. As I stood there, I was suddenly overwhelmed by the strongest smell of hyacinths, there were half a dozen of them, growing in pots in the garden, but it was such a strange thing to happen, as there was no breeze whatsoever, but the fragrance was so heavy in the air, that it literally caught my breath for a few moments. I looked down to see that Luna was still beside me, but had settled herself down on the step of Dan's cabin, so I sat on the floor next to her and with my back against his door and for over an hour in the quiet darkness, I cried.

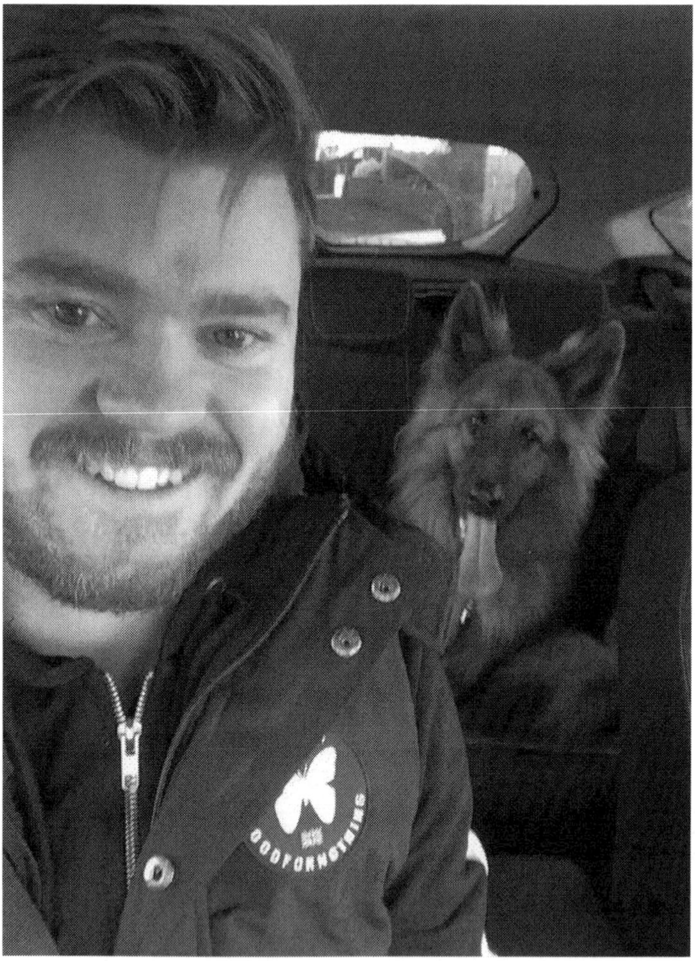

Drifting Through the Days

Now, Danny had never really lived his life in what some may say, a predicable manner or what others would class as, normal. So for us as a family to suddenly have to accept that he had just died in his sleep for no visibly obvious or apparent reason just because it happens, or is one of those things, would have been totally ignorant on our part and completely out of character for him. I needed a reason, everyone dies for a reason and nobody this young, fit and healthy with such a love for life just closes their eyes and dies. If he had been ill, killed in an accident, murdered or even took his own life, at least there would be something or someone to blame. Not to make it acceptable, but at the very least, make it slightly more understandable, but we had nothing and the reality that brought with Danny's tragic and unbelievably abrupt end was just too excruciating to deal with. I had only been talking to him in the garden six or so hours before he had died. Nothing was wrong with him, at all. He had been to work, come home and gone to the gym and believe me, if Danny had felt the slightest bit unwell he would never have gone there. Those last hours just kept going over and over in my head, after the gym, he had taken Luna for a walk using the new lead he had bought her, then complaining how she had 'been a nightmare at walking and pulling the whole time'. I passed him in the hallway and said, "Don't worry babe, she'll get used to it", patting him on the shoulder and laughing. That was the last thing I ever said to Danny and the last time I saw him alive. He sat with Rich and had his dinner then went to watch football in his room. He had spent the rest of the evening talking to Meg, texting his friends and playing PS4 online until just after 11pm.

How had this happened? You cannot begin to imagine that family life can be decimated forever in such a short space of time, with no apparent cause. There was a constant thought playing in my head, going over and over saying, 'He won't understand what has happened, he'll be lost. He wouldn't have known as he lay down, that he was never going to wake up and see us all again". It was pure torture. Did we have to accept his life had been blown out like a candle and that was that? Being left heartbroken beyond repair and with absolutely nothing to vent your pain, anger and frustration at is indescribably unbearable. I just needed something, anything that would actually make me face the fact that he had died. We all desperately needed some kind of explanation as to why this had happened to our family. The following day, our home was once again filled with family and friends. People were coming and going and flowers were being delivered hourly. It didn't take long before every available shelf, window sill, table and sizable area of flooring was host to a large bouquet of flowers. Visitors didn't really have any words, everyone just sat in a silence of disbelief. I was sitting upstairs on my bed when my brother Dean and sister in law arrived, he walked in, we didn't speak, he just sat down beside me, held me tight and we cried.

It was the day before my 50th birthday and shortly after Dean had arrived, Becky nervously appeared at the bedroom door with a birthday gift. This had been delivered on the Thursday to a neighbour, as the postman had arrived whilst the paramedics were running into the house. Becky gave me this small box which contained the most beautiful, silver pendant necklace from the children, with all of their names engraved upon it. I really started to cry upon seeing this, all five of my children, their names linked together on this delicate piece of jewellery and something that had only been discussed amongst them and ordered a few days before. How could life change so quickly? My perfect five, they were always together yet it had taken only a moment in time to cruelly separate them forever, Dan was gone but there on the necklace that I held in my hand was his name, perfectly engraved alongside his brothers and sisters.

During the afternoon, so many of Danny's friends turned up on the doorstep. I can't recall how many of them there were as they filed into the house and one by one, took it in turns to give me a hug. The lounge was quickly filled and with no sofa space for anyone to sit, they just sat down on the floor and all began to crying uncontrollably. I remember looking at them all heartbroken and devastated by the sudden loss of their best mate and thinking of all those times previously that this amazing group of friends had walked through our front door, bypassing this room en route to Dan's cabin for a games night in or when they had waited in the hallway for him to come rushing up because they were off out somewhere. Seeing all his lifelong friends sitting here now, so emotionally traumatised was beyond heartbreaking. Dan's death wasn't a ripple effect on a few, it was a tsunami of destruction for so many lives and it really made me realise the magnitude of Danny's popularity and how deeply loved he was by so many.

On the Saturday, my 50th birthday came and went completely un-acknowledged. I don't recall us having as many visitors that day, but in the evening Rich took our youngest two children to stay with their auntie for the night. Whilst he was gone Dan's Meg and I looked at his and hers, matching wedding rings. She found the design that she liked and chose the perfect inscription to go on the inside of each one before we placed the order. Meg was Dan's forever love and I know that if they had been given more time, they would have got married and had a family of their own. This was the smallest of gestures, but at least now, as soon as we heard from the coroner that we could go and see Danny, Meg would be able to put a wedding ring on him.

It took a week for us to hear from the coroner and this is where a whole new nightmare started to unfold for us. The outcome of Danny's post mortem was recorded as 'unexplained death'. I was told by the coroner that in order for them to allow Danny to be returned to us for his funeral plans to be made, I would have to agree to his heart being removed from him indefinitely as it had to be sent to a hospital in London for further investigation. If we wanted his heart to be reunited with him after the investigations, which she told me could take six months, then Danny would have to remain where he was, meaning no funeral could take place. This was a horrendous decision to have to make. I didn't want my son being pulled about, let alone separated from his heart but neither could I stand the thought of him laying there in a mortuary for what could possibly be months whilst the cause of death was investigated. I wanted him back; Meg and Steven hadn't seen Danny and wanted to spend some time with him. Yet again, the clock kept ticking and the longer he remained where he was, the smaller the window of opportunity for them to see him became. I wanted him somewhere he could be taken care of and as a family; we could start making arrangements for his 'Day'. I gave my consent for his heart to be removed and asked the coroner for the name of the hospital and to whom his heart was being sent, she gave me both. I searched the information given and found out that St George's Tooting was the main research clinic in the country which investigates the cause of death in those with possible undiagnosed cardiac arrhythmias. I also looked up the name of the professor on the internet as I wanted to put a face to the person who was to have the responsibility of taking care of something so very precious and this is where our journey with Cardiac Risk in the Young began.

The Chapel of Rest

On Friday 17th March, we were told that Danny could be released back to us and the undertakers that we had chosen to take care of him, went to collect him from the hospital where he had been for just over a week. I had given them clothes for Danny, a brand new West Ham polo top that his Dad had bought him for his birthday, Armani boxer shorts, claret and blue Ralph Lauren socks and his favourite Levi jeans. He also had a West Ham scarf which Meg's mum had bought for him. The undertaker told us we could go and see Danny after 1pm that afternoon.

Meg hadn't seen Danny since Monday 6th March, when he had taken her to Euston station for her journey back to Liverpool. They didn't have very long as Dan was on his way to work, but he had seen her safely onto the train and hugged and kissed her goodbye before having to rush off. Unknowingly to them both, those last few precious moments together, that final kiss and cuddle that they shared, were the last they would ever have.

Meg was totally destroyed and needed to see him. I think maybe to prove that this horrendous nightmare we were now all living, had actually happened. Being so surreal and so unbelievable, it does become a 'need to see it, to believe it' situation. Steven had been unable to go into Danny's room and see him when he had rushed home from London after I had phoned him, and although was still unsure of what to do, he decided he would go and if he felt he could, he would say goodbye to his younger brother at the chapel. Richard had spent a long time with Danny in his room on the day we lost him and had decided he didn't want to see him again, especially now he was in the chapel, but he wanted to drive me and Meg there, whilst Steven followed behind with Becky in his car.

We arrived just after 1pm and as soon as we walked through the doors into the funeral home, I started to cry, I felt sick and faint. Trying to compose myself, I was taking in every tiny detail of the unfamiliar surroundings as the five of us stood huddled together in the corridor. It was silent, there were painted doves on the ceiling, leaflets on tables and a few vases of silk flower arrangements, a blue carpet with a tiny pattern in it, the pale blue and cream walls with ornate coving seemed magnified as I stood there trying to accept I was actually where I was. A lady in a blue suit came along and asked us to follow her. Walking with her, we passed comfy looking chairs in groups of two positioned outside the doors to different chapels as we began our way towards the room which held our precious Danny. I knew that behind each of these doors was someone's lost loved one. The doors had names of places on them; each chapel named, all except the one we were walking towards, the last one at the end of the corridor, this had nothing written on it. We all stopped; facing us was a big fish tank with large goldfish swimming around in it, but for a rather sickly looking one which was drifting about at the bottom. The lady turned towards the closed and un-named door to her left and began to open it.

The room was dark inside and she leaned in and turned on softly dimmed wall lights. There, right in the middle of the room was a heavy cloth covered metal trolley and resting upon that was an open claret and blue coloured coffin. I was stunned and felt paralysed by the sight and couldn't move at all. I just momentarily stared into the room and all I could see was the top of Danny's hair and part of his forehead lying within the casket. Suddenly my focus was broken by the sound of Meg crying hysterically. She was to my left but slightly behind me. I spun around and grabbed hold of her as her legs were giving way and she was heading towards the floor, pulling her up towards me, she buried her face into my chest. I could see Steven and Becky both crying and backing away down the corridor in the direction to which we had just come. I turned to Richard; he was crying and standing by the door to the chapel but rushed over and put his arms around me and helped to support Meg. I don't know how many seconds, or whether it was minutes that passed as we stood within that emotional chaos of being no longer together, but divided into two little groups, before I started to walk into the room, facing yet another unimaginable and unbelievable sight of my beautiful young son, laying in a bespoke West Ham coffin.

I couldn't take any of it in, yet instantly, my eyes were drawn to the corner of the room where against the wall, beside a chair stood the lid of the coffin. This was such a shocking sight as it had the printed image of a West Ham shirt with 'DANNY 25' emblazoned across the front of it. Now, with just the three of us standing in the doorway, we slowly started to walk in towards Danny. Upon reaching him, I pulled back the thin mesh cloth that was draped over the top of the coffin and threw it onto the chair. And there we stood, completely destroyed and heartbroken and in total silence looking at Danny just lying there, so unnaturally still and quiet. That once beautiful and amazing smile now gone forever, only to have been replaced with what I can only describe as, the grumpiest look I had seen on his face since he was a little boy.

They had styled his hair all wrong and I could hear him saying to me "Mum, sort it out, my hair looks criminal". I pushed back his soft auburn fringe; it moved so freely and thankfully, stayed in place. I know he would have been pleased about how it was now. I said to Meg, "If it falls forward again, we will have to bring some gel in tomorrow". She nodded, but didn't speak, she just stood there looking at him and she was beyond heartbroken and looked so totally lost. Tears were running down her face, I felt completely destroyed for her and for Danny. They had their lives mapped out together and absolutely everything going for them. Only two weeks earlier they had been busy arranging their holidays for the year ahead and now he was gone, ripped away from her, their future just obliterated over night and there was nothing any of us could do to change it. This was truly the most heart-rending thing to witness, this beautiful young woman, standing there beside her forever love, lost in thought and gently stroking his face and hands.

Steven and Becky were now standing back by the door and both walked in towards their brother. I can't recall how long Steve and Beck were in with Dan, but we all got to spend some personal time alone with him. I didn't think it looked like Danny. I knew it was him but as I stood there stroking his face, all I could see was a shell that had once been home to the kindest, most loving and caring son, brother, boyfriend, grandson and friend, our spontaneous and fun loving Danny for 25 years and six days. That life force, that spirit, that beauty within him had gone and all that was here in front of me now was the shell of that amazing, unique and extra-ordinary child of mine.

I placed a few photos and letters from myself, Rich, Megan and Regan in with him. In his arms, I laid the threadbare white rabbit named 'Bun-Bun' which Dan had been completely inseparable from throughout his early childhood and had been stored safely in the loft for over twenty years. Danny had loved this little rabbit so much and always had it with him wherever he went, right up until he started school. He had hugged, rubbed, kissed and loved the little sewn face off this rabbit on quite a few occasions, giving need for me to take it from him when he slept and quickly reconstruct a new threaded nose and eyes, before he woke and noticed it missing! The other item I placed alongside him was a soft red velvet heart. I had bought one, each for Dan and Steve, about fifteen years ago on Valentine's Day. As Danny no longer had his own heart with him, I felt this was the only option available and as it had been hanging in his room since I had given it to him all those years ago, it should be this heart that would now lay alongside him forever.

I knew once I walked out of the chapel, I would not go back in again. This really was it, the last time I would ever look at him, be able to touch him and kiss him. I had had my time with Dan, I'd spent half my life with him and he'd spent all of his with me. Meg needed her time with him now and I wanted the last person ever to kiss him and see him, to be his forever love. So, I stroked his face one last time, leant over and gently whispered "I will love you forever my darling, precious boy", before kissing him on the forehead and leaving the room and the two of them alone.

West Ham - Saturday, 18th March

Steven and one of Dan's best mates Grant had been sharing Danny's tragic story on social media in the week following his death. They were pushing for West Ham to do a minute of applause during the home game against Leicester the following Saturday. Our local newspaper had also picked up on the story and was encouraging the public and fans to get behind it. It was shared across Twitter and Facebook over a thousand times, the response was absolutely phenomenal. A couple of days before, West Ham got in touch and said they would read out a tribute to Danny just before kickoff and display a picture of him on the screen as well as putting it in the programme. They said that due to the vast number of tributes and birthdays they are asked to acknowledge, they would no longer be doing them weekly, but would remember fans and celebrate birthdays in groups a couple of times a year going forward. This meant that Danny's tribute on the screen would be the last individual one they were prepared to do. They also added that unfortunately they no longer did a minute of applause during any games.

On Saturday 18th March we all attended the game and as promised, many friends who didn't have season tickets attended the match just to be part of the tribute to him. Many had bought West Ham shirts and had Danny 25 printed on the back. We all had white T shirts with Danny's picture on the front and Danny 25 on the back. Just before kickoff, a picture of my smiling son with his name above it was displayed on the huge stadium screen. I wasn't really prepared for it as it came up, so it was quite a shocking and heartbreaking sight. The tribute was lovely and extremely emotional for all his family and friends who were there. Danny had been a season ticket holder for many years and had only been at the West Ham v Chelsea game three days before he died so most people who sat in the vicinity of his seat and knew him were completely devastated to hear what had happened. I struggled to remain emotionally composed during the match as it wasn't the place I wanted to be just a week after losing my son. I kept thinking how he would have been here, sitting in his seat alongside Steve and Grant, doing his usual cheering, swearing and moaning at the players but instead, Meg was sitting in his seat and he was lying in a chapel of rest. As the game hit the twenty-fifth minute of play, fans all around the stadium started to clap. It was like a Mexican wave of applause that rippled around the stadium, from row to row and from front to back. The fans were all on their feet applauding my son. Even the Leicester fans were clapping. People all around shouting out 'For Danny, clap for Danny'. It was surreal, just like each of the days before but something none of us will ever forget and in hindsight, I'm glad we went and that we were a part of, it was amazing to witness and tremendously emotional, Danny would have loved it.

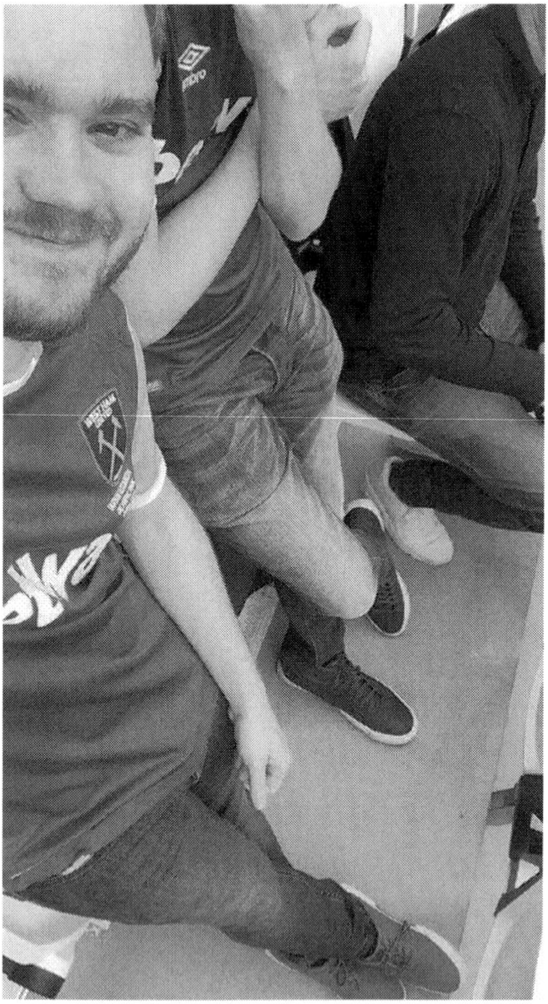

The Missing Butterfly

After the Friday visit, made with the family to see Danny in the chapel of rest, I had decided that I did not want to go back and see him again. I knew Dan wouldn't have wanted people coming to see him. All of our immediate family and the closest of his friends had been told that there was a 'time window' of just two days to visit him and should they wish to leave any photos or letters in with him, then this would be the only opportunity to do so. On the morning of Saturday 18th March, before we left for the West Ham game, a couple of Danny's friends went to see him and shortly after they had left, Richard drove Meg back to spend some final time with Danny. I told Rich, that when Meg came out of the chapel, he was to ask the undertakers to close the coffin and that no one else was to see him. The matching rings that had been ordered the week before had arrived and this allowed Meg to place the wedding ring that she had chosen for Dan, upon his finger. During the following week, Meg was feeling unwell and decided she would return to Liverpool and come back prior to 'Danny's Day'.

The house was so suppressing and heartbreakingly empty; everything in it was a constant reminder of that one person who was now forever missing. Although there was a steady stream of visitors, this just magnified Danny's absence all the more. My heart was smashed into a million pieces and my emotions were all over the place. I didn't really eat much and sleeping for any length of time was impossible. I wanted more than anything to have the ability to focus on my other four, completely devastated children, but I just couldn't. I am so ashamed to say, that at that point in time, nothing helped divert my downward spiralling emotional state away from the loss of Dan, not even the love I have for his siblings, even though their own visibly obvious needs screamed out at me every time I looked at them. I had completely shut down and Rich was really worried, so a doctor's appointment was booked and some Diazepam was prescribed to be taken when needed!

I have never really been one to take tablets or medicines unless they have been completely necessary, so to suddenly be faced with the 'take when required' diagnosis, I felt this was the beginning of a drug dependent way of dragging myself through each day, for the rest of my life. I had only been prescribed 15 tablets but hoped that when the next emotional episode began to well up within me, I might be able to get through it in a more controlled way. Regan had started referring to my debilitating attacks of grief as 'Having a moment'. I certainly did feel that taking a tablet did make the jagged edge of pain feel a little less excruciating. I was also though very aware that if I took one every time I began to cry uncontrollably, these little white pills of numbness were possibly only going to last me three days at the most. So with that in mind, I decided that I when I felt I needed the 'edge' being taken off a particularly worse 'Moment', I'd have half of one and see how things went. This worked quite well, plus they were more helpful to me when I was struggling emotionally at night whilst trying to get some sleep.

It had been over ten days since I had been to the Chapel of Rest. I woke up on 28th March in a complete mess. I had the most overwhelming feeling of guilt because Danny had been left lying there all alone in that Chapel for such a long time. It was only a week to go until 'Danny's Day' and I asked Rich to take me to the chapel as I wanted to sit with him now and every day until his funeral. The vicious reality hit me that this really was the last chance I would ever have to be physically close to my son. We got dressed and rang the undertakers to tell them that we would be coming in to spend time with Dan. The week before Dan passed away, he had asked his Meg if she would order and collect a pair of Michael Kors earrings that he wanted to get me for my birthday. She had done this and brought them with her when she came down the night he had died, giving them to me on my birthday, just as Dan had wanted. These earrings are the most precious piece of jewellery that I have, and so deciding where and when they will be worn, will always be very carefully thought about first. I considered the fact that as we were going in the car and would be inside the chapel for the whole time whilst I spent time with Danny, I decided I wanted to wear the earrings whilst I was with him. So this was the first time they were ever worn.

We arrived at the chapel mid-morning and I spent a few hours sitting in the un-named room with him. Rich appeared a few times at the door to check I was OK, but returned to sit outside in the corridor. On one occasion he asked if I wanted a cup of tea as one of the staff had offered. I came out of the chapel and sat with Rich and a lovely lady called Anne, telling her all about our beautiful and amazing son, who was lying just a few feet away. As we finished our tea, Rich noticed that one of my earrings was hanging loosely from my ear. I put my hand up and realised that the butterfly was missing from the back. Panic set in as I jumped up and we all started looking at the floor around where we were sitting. It wasn't there. Anne suggested that it had probably come loose whilst I had been in with Dan, so back into the chapel I went to find it. I was looking around the blue carpeted room and the chair in which I had been sitting, around the skirting boards and by the door but couldn't see it at anywhere. I was beginning to get upset and so I said to Danny, "Please babe, help me find it, I know it's got to be here. Please, please help me." Danny's coffin was resting upon a heavy cloth covered trolley, I thought that maybe the small and round, silver butterfly could have rolled underneath it. I got down onto my hands and knees and proceeded to circle the trolley which held the coffin that contained my precious child, whilst patting my hand on the floor underneath it, in the hope of finding the butterfly! It was during the second rotation of Danny, at the end where his head was, that I stopped and looked up at the six foot claret and blue coffin and could easily visualize Danny laughing hysterically and saying "Mum, what the bloody hell are you doing?!!" I quickly started glancing up at the ceiling for a security camera, thinking how totally mad I must look crawling around on my hands and knees in this chapel of rest! My moment of surveillance was interrupted as I was aware that the door was now open. Peering under the trolley, I couldn't see any feet, so I stretched up on my knees and popped my head above the top end of Dan's coffin. Richard was leaning against the door frame with his hand over his mouth laughing hysterically through his nose while literally trying to hold in as much sound as was physically possible before saying, "Babe, what on earth are you doing?" I also started to laugh and quickly jumped to my feet and headed for the door. I said, "I can't find the butterfly, it's not here and they are different to any other earring backs that I have." I was way beyond upset and as I walked down the corridor and I said to Rich that I would meet him outside.

Waiting there on the pavement by the main road and with my heart racing and tears streaming down my face, I apologised to Danny in my head for losing the back to one of the earrings he had bought me. I really don't' know what made me stop where I did, nor what made me look down directly in front of where I was standing, but something did and there in a tiny gap between two block paving stones was the small and round, silver back to my earring. I was astonished and quickly picked it up, just as Richard walked out. "I've found it!" I shouted, "I can't believe it, it has been stuck in between the paving stones since we went in!"

As we walked back to our car and I looked up to the sky and just knew that Danny was with us and that he had somehow helped direct me outside to find the missing butterfly.

Danny's Day

Tuesday 4th April 2017 was Danny's Day. I would not refer it as his funeral and so from the first point of making the arrangements and even the printing on the order of service sheets, it was referred to as 'Danny's Day'. I didn't want there to be anything religious about the service for him, and as a family we had all agreed that this is what Dan himself would want and so a humanist called Jay was chosen to conduct it for us. Both of Richard's parents had worked locally within the funeral business all their working lives, so we were very fortunate that those who had taken care of Danny right from the start and who were now helping us through this unimaginably difficult period, were close friends of theirs and treated us all, including Dan, like family. We had discussed with a large group of his friends that his 'Day' was going to be completely personal, those attending were to wear bright colours to reflect Danny's personality and all tributes would be made by anyone who wanted to say something or share a story. Needless to say, everyone wanted to play a part for their friend on the day.

I didn't really sleep at all during the night and got up just after 5am, went downstairs and curled up into a ball on the sofa in the lounge and just cried. Richard came down an hour or so later and we didn't speak, we just held one another and continued to cry together. I had arranged with Dan's Meg to go to the Chapel of Rest just after 8am and for the last time to spend a couple of hours sitting with him. Whilst getting ready, I heard a car pull up outside and the gate open, I walked over to the window and watched as the first of many floral tributes were gently placed in our front garden. Meg and I left the house and when we returned, many more flowers had arrived, leaving little space in the garden. There was a two foot high Coke Cola can – made up of red and white flowers, alongside a two foot wide, white chrysanthemum 'XBOX' controller, from his friends. A large claret and blue flower West Ham shirt was there, it had 'Danny 25' written across the front of it. There was a flower football and lots of wreaths and hand tied bouquets that had been left. Two large floral tributes on stands were also there, one was from Steven, it was the crossed hammers West Ham logo, with the word 'Brother' written on it and the other was the Australian flag, sent from family who had met Dan whilst he was there.

The service wasn't until 3.20pm and we had booked the last two slots of the day at the crematorium which would allow plenty of time for everyone to speak and the video tributes to be played, without having to worry about another funeral taking place after Danny's. The Undertakers were coming at 2.15pm to give time to place floral arrangements on the cars and allow enough time to drive the procession past Dan's school and through the town centre where he had spent many enjoyable times during his life. His friends were all going directly to the crematorium, as I had asked them to form a Guard of Honour both sides of the entrance for Dan's arrival. Family slowly started turning up at our house, I was trying to get ready and couldn't stomach the speed at which the day was moving, so kept to myself for as long as possible. When I came downstairs, I was shocked by the amount of people who were sporadically dotted around the house. The lounge was full, as was the dining room and kitchen. The front door was wide open and people were standing in the hallway and spilling out onto the front path. Thankfully, it wasn't raining but there was a thick blanket of grey cloud covering the sky. You could no longer walk amongst the floral tributes and considering the amount of people, there was an uncomfortable silence which was occasionally broken by a muffled comment about the flowers. I stood in the dining room and started to shake and feel sick, I had never had a panic attack before but suddenly my heart was pounding and I thought I was going to pass out, hurrying to the kitchen I downed a glass of water with a Diazepam tablet. I was really losing control at this point and kept asking Richard if Danny was outside. I didn't want this to become any more real than it already was. I didn't want the hearse carrying my son, pulling up outside our home where only a few weeks ago he had parked his car. I kept asking and Rich kept saying "No babe, he's not here yet". I couldn't leave the dining room and started saying to those standing near me "I can't do this, I just can't do this", but no one had any words of comfort, they themselves all looked so helpless and lost. I'm not sure exactly how long had passed when the inaudible whispering stopped and Richard walked back in to the dining room towards me, his face was ashen and following behind him, suited, booted, carrying a cane and wearing a top hat, was the conducting undertaker. Danny was here.

Once again I began to shake and cry uncontrollably. Johnny, (the undertaker) took off his hat and held my hands and told me to take long deep breaths, reassuring me that we had all the time we wanted and that there was no rush. But we didn't have time, time had run out and after a few minutes we walked into the hallway. All I could see, looking directly through a corridor of faces and beyond the open front door was the hearse carrying the claret and blue coffin, which within it, held my precious boy. It was as though everyone suddenly disappeared as I walked outside. I remember standing at the back of the hearse with Richard and facing a large, beautiful colour framed photo of Danny smiling back at us. I could see four or five limousine drivers placing the flower tributes on the hearse and around Dan, but don't recall anyone else standing near. Soon enough, we were all ushered into the cars which slowly pulled away from our home. Richard had asked if he and Regan could walk in front of Danny, down our road with Johnny as we left and it was at this moment that I noticed neighbours all along both sides of our road, standing at their windows and at front doors watching as we drove past. I was in the front car with Becky, Megan, Meg, Steve and once we reached the end of our road, Regan and Rich got in. Regan had to sit shot-gun with the driver, which made him feel very special and important but to me, I tried to imagine what must have been going through that little boy's mind. He just looked so small and sad sitting there on his own at the front of the limo, following his beloved brother to the crematorium.

The procession stopped about twenty metres from the entrance to the grounds of the crematorium and once again, Rich and Regan took their place alongside John and began walking in front of Danny. As the cars turned in, there standing shoulder to shoulder and on either sides of the entrance were the closest of Danny's friends, some were in tears and others just looking like they were still in complete disbelief at actually being there, but all united in forming the most perfect guard of honour for their best friend.

There was a sea of people standing outside the south chapel of the crematorium. The car doors were opened and we all got out and stood like rabbits caught in headlights, not sure which way to turn or where to go. Regan was standing all alone under a canopy outside the chapel and he looked completely lost and bewildered by his surroundings. John asked if I wanted to go into a side room with the children, but I said no. I couldn't quite take in that this was all actually real as the back of the hearse opened and I watched as Rich and Steve, friends Grant and Jimmy, Danny's other brother Ricky and his Dad took up their positions either side of the hearse and gently lifted Danny up and onto their shoulders.

The chapel seats 150 but was filled to bursting point. There must have been over 200 people there as every seat was taken and the aisles and sides of the crematorium were filled by those standing. Angels by Robbie Williams started to play and as if in slow motion, Danny was carried in and with tears streaming down their faces, his bearers carefully placed him at the front.

And so it started, here we all were at Danny's funeral. A poem was read out by the humanist taking the service and then I got up to give my own tribute to my beautiful son. It was such a cloudy and grey day, but apparently as I started to speak, the sun came out and shone through a window behind me, casting its light across my head and shining onto Danny. I was completely unaware of this at the time, but after leaving the service lots of people came up to me and said how perfectly timed and beautiful it was when it happened. Dan's dad also made a tribute and this was followed by a video of photos and video clips, set to the music of 'I Lived' by One Republic and 'Fix You' by Coldplay. Everyone was in tears after this finished and it was at this point that ten of his best friends, who had proudly stood beside his casket throughout the 80 minute service, began their own verbal tribute for him. They spoke for over 30 minutes and shared funny stories and memories that they had made with Dan over the years. It was a true testament to Danny of the love and friendship that he had given and received throughout his short life. It really was something else to have nearly 200 people singing 'I'm forever blowing bubbles' and it made this service for Dan so special and unique, just like him because it was filled from start to finish, not just with tears of sadness, but with lots of spontaneous laughter at the hilarious escapades that he had got up too and the comical situations he had found himself in and the amazing experiences he had enjoyed with so many. We had another video tribute of more photos and videos before the service reached its conclusion, and in typical Dan style, his favourite tune by Westlife was chosen, 'When you're looking like that'.

Danny's Day was finished with Steven playing his guitar and singing one of his favourite Green Day songs, 'Time of your Life'. Steve was extremely nervous about doing this, not sure if he would actually be able to sing and play in such distressing circumstances but oh boy, did that son of mine and that devoted big brother, do Danny proud. It was heartbreakingly perfect as Steven sung his brother out, and when the majority of those there, who knew the words, started to sing along in support, once again the tears of so many began to flow. It was a beautiful send off which was personal and bespoke to Danny. I had asked that the curtain not be pulled around Dan, I wanted us to walk out and be able to glance back and him still be there rather than the alternative. Dan's Meg, Joanne and Chris had spent the week prior to this day, making keepsake feathers to be given to all of those who attended his day. Between them, they had tied tiny claret and blue ribbons around the quill end of two hundred, finger sized white feathers, which the undertakers handed out as people left the crematorium. We walked out last and headed over to where they had placed Danny's flower tributes and lined up to release the doves. The lady handed out a dove to each of us that wanted to release one; Becky was holding hers a little too tight and was asked if she would quickly loosen her grip, before she threw it up into the air, just so that it could catch its breath…..that caused a ripple of laughter at the thought of the consequences! The lady then said a few words about how releasing the doves symbolised Danny flying freely up to heaven and it was at this point that a gently breeze of wind blew through the branches of the flowering cherry blossom trees behind us, and literally showered us with natures, pink petal confetti. For those watching remarked how beautiful it looked from where they were standing.

We had booked a function room at our local bowls club and everyone headed there after we left the crematorium. We spent over five hours there, making conversation and honouring Danny. It was a wonderful send off for him and the celebration of his life came to its conclusion, just after 11pm with a round of 'Sambuka shots'. It was the most fitting toast for this kind, happy and fun loving individual, who had always embraced life and what it had to offer by grabbing each precious moment he had been given and living it to the full.

A Handful of Ashes

For a couple of weeks since Danny's Day, there had been quite a few conversations as to what should happen with his ashes and where they should be placed. Although it had been mentioned by some, that the ashes be scattered or should go into his own plot, I would not consider either of these options for him. There was no way Danny was going to be placed on his own in a corner of the cemetery and neither was he being scattered, denying him a private memorial of his existence. So after a discussion with the family, we agreed that his ashes be interred in my Dad's grave. It is fair to say, I would have brought his ashes home with me, but I knew that was a purely selfish decision and completely unfair to his friends and his Dad if they should ever want to go and place flowers or spend some time with him. A few days before his funeral, I had asked the undertakers for three locks of Danny's hair and if it would be possible for me to have a small amount of his ashes held back, before they were finally sealed in the West Ham ash box prior to his interment, which was arranged for the afternoon of Friday 28th April.

On Wednesday 26th April, Ann (Richard's mum), rang to say that Danny's ashes had arrived back at the crematorium. She said she did not want to leave him at the crematorium on his own for the two days until interment and wondered if we minded her taking them home with her. We were in the car when Rich got the call and he pulled over and told me what she had suggested. I burst into tears and said Dan was not to be left in the offices for two days but that I felt I wanted him to be in his own home for what would be the last time ever that he could. We were worried how Megan and Regan would feel about knowing they were there, if we brought them home and let them be in the cabin until Friday. I said I would rather deal with the consequences of any upset from them both rather than not bringing his ashes home and never having that chance again. I said I thought Danny would want to come home rather than being at Rich's mum and dad's, but was so upset I really didn't know what to do and said to Rich "What shall we do, what would Danny want?". Rich said "Let's drive up to the crematorium and make a decision when we are there babe". He said "If you want to take Danny back to my mums and sit there with him all night, then that's what we'll do. You can make a decision later, let's just go and see how you feel". I was really crying, not at the thought of what to do with my son's ashes, but just the awful reality of the situation. Richard turned the car engine back on and we started heading off to the Crematorium. The news was on the radio as we drove off and this finished literally a minute into our journey, being replaced with Coldplay's, 'Fix you'. We looked at each other and Rich instantly burst into tears, so now we were both crying and continued to cry until we reached our destination and 'Fix you' finished as we drove through the gates of the Crematorium. This was all the sign I needed, this was confirmation that Danny wanted to come home for the last two nights before his ashes were laid to rest with his beloved Grandad for always.

We walked into the offices of the crematorium and Ann took us into a side room and we sat down. There was a large cardboard box, which she carefully opened and slowly lifted out a small wooden claret and blue, West Ham ashes box and handed it to me. I started to cry hysterically as I looked at Dan's name and the dates that were printed on the top of this small but quite heavy wooden box. I couldn't catch my breath and was practically screaming, when Ann just wrapped her arms around me until I had cried out the shock. It took a good few minutes to compose myself and with the box containing Danny's ashes now resting on my lap, I looked up at Ann standing in front of me holding a little blue velvet pouch. She didn't speak but lifted my hand and gently placed it onto my palm.

There were no more emotions left in me to give at that moment as I stared at that little Navy blue velvet pouch. This was Danny, this was all that was left of my perfect, amazing, clever, kind and beautiful son, who had been taken from us so suddenly, just as his adult life was beginning. Everything that he had meant to his family and to so many others was over, and now all we were left with was a million memories and irreparable broken hearts. Once again I began to cry, my mind was blank, my own memories were lost within an ocean of grief and my own broken heart just ached through being separated from Danny. I had held that boy in my arms all of his life and now all I had of my child was contained within this little blue velvet pouch, feeling tragically destroyed, I just sat there in complete silence staring and holding this very precious handful of ashes.

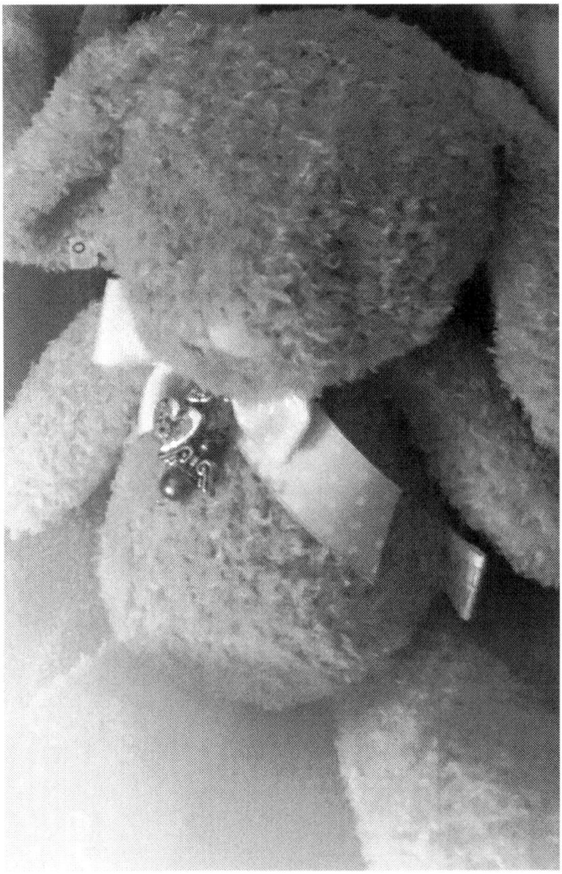

Out of the Blue

On Tuesday 23rd May, I unexpectedly received a phone call to say that the final autopsy report for Danny had been completed. This report had no relation to the investigations that were being carried out on his heart by St George's Hospital in London, it only confirmed that he had died by natural causes and that nothing specifically had been found.

A few days after the telephone call from the coroner's office, I received the post mortem report through the post. I cannot begin to explain what a horrific shock this was. I never realised that these reports were sent directly to the family and if I had known or been informed of its contents and the graphic account of what had been done to my child during this process, I would never have read it. I will live with the regret of reading this report for the rest of my life, but it had arrived unexpectedly and was about my son and so I couldn't stop myself from reading every page of the clinically blunt account of what they had done to him. The first sentence started with 'This 25 year old well nourished, bearded Caucasian male ....', this was Danny they were referring to, yet apart from his name at the top of the document, there was no further reference to him as a person, just a graphically descriptive investigative report of a dead body. I cried and shook as I read through it. I had the most horrendous images in my head which were so bad, I could actually picture him laying there and watching it happen with my own eyes. How could I have been so naive? Was I really that stupid to believe that they had only removed his heart? I genuinely thought that nothing else had been done other than taking blood samples to rule out drugs and alcohol, as the circumstances surrounding his death had shown from the very beginning that there was nothing sinister about it. But this is not how it works; he had passed away in his sleep with no warning, illness or reason. They had analysed absolutely everything and when they had done this and come up with nothing, they were sure it was something genetic within his heart and why it was sent away. I would say to anyone who may read this book, take it from a mother who now knows, never read a post mortem report of a loved one.

Ultimately, the report findings gave the cause of death as Sudden Arrhythmic Death Syndrome and this information finally allowed me to register and obtain a death certificate for Dan. It was difficult to accept that Danny had died because he had an unknown arrhythmia which had caused his heart to stop beating while he slept. SADS is an umbrella term broadly used when a specific cause of heart defect or arrhythmia cannot be found. Within two months of Dan passing away and alongside hundreds of other families, we were all walking in Dan's memory across six of London's Bridges raising awareness and funds for the charity CRY. Although we only had very little by way of the reason why Dan was no longer with us, we shared something with all of these other families as they also had lost young, fit and healthy loved ones in such unexplained and tragic circumstances. There are many arrhythmias that affect the heart and the one that they believed was possibly responsible for taking Danny is known as Brugada Syndrome. This arrhythmia is undetectable once a heart has stopped beating and the only way this can be confirmed for certain is to test all immediate family members to see if they carry the defective gene. We had to wait a couple of months but an appointment was made for each of us to attend St George's hospital in London on Wednesday August 16th.

The Psychic Night

On 2nd July 2017, my friend Tracy and I booked up to go and see a local psychic show. It was only a short distance from home and something that we have both always been interested in and visited before. Obviously being so close to Danny's passing, I felt quite anxious about it, not because I hoped for a message but I have always believed that when you die, you do go to a higher plain, so was more worried that to hear something directed towards someone else in the audience, or if Danny wasn't there, I'd maybe begin to question my belief in life after life. I don't believe in God, so I never imagined white pearly gates with some bearded older guy sitting on a chair with a register, telling recently departed souls, who could and who couldn't come in! I have though had many strange things happen in my life, which over the years has confirmed to me that death isn't the end, more the beginning of another journey.   Tracy told me not to expect too much because she had been to many of these 'audience' shows and as there can be about 200 people in attendance, it was very unlikely that a message would come through. She said she had never been given a direct message from a loved one, other than at a private one to one sitting.

Steven and his girlfriend Nicole had only flown back from the holiday that the four of them had intended to take to America, the week before and so I told Steven and Becky that I was going to a psychic night. It also just happened that the same weekend as the show, Meg was coming down for a few days and she and Becky decided they wanted to come with Tracy and me. Steven said he didn't think it was for him but on the morning of the show, he rang and was quite intrigued as to what it would all be like. I said to him to that he could come along and pay on the door and if he changed his mind, then he didn't have to come and it wouldn't have cost him anything. He said he would have a think about it but within half hour, he'd messaged me back to say he and Nic would probably meet us there.

The four of us that were confirmed, all headed off just after 6pm in time for the 7pm start. We sat in the large hall waiting for the Psychic to begin, when Steve and Nic walked in and took up seats next to us. I would reckon that there were about 150 people there. The lady medium came out and the evening started. There was lots of message's coming through for various groups and individuals dotted about the hall. It is a very emotional and sensitive experience watching and listening to people receive a message from a loved one who has passed over. I looked at Steven on a few occasions and he sat there listening but had a bit of an unconvinced facial expression for most of it. There was an interval and then the evening resumed but was now running fifteen minutes off schedule. The clairvoyant said that there were quite a few waiting to make contact with loved ones in the audience and that if it was OK with us, she'd run over the difference at the end as she wanted to pass on all the messages if she could.

The clairvoyant was halfway through the second half when I noticed that the silver locket I was wearing was feeling very warm, on the point of being hot. The locket contains a small picture of Danny and a lock of his hair. I am very careful where I wear it as I am constantly fearful that it will fall off or get caught and I'd lose it. For this reason, I had the locket on the inside of my top and it was tucked into my bra! Hence how I was suddenly aware that it was becoming warm! I know this must sound totally ridiculous and to be honest, if I was a non-believer and was hearing all this, I'd be a little sceptical!! Anyway, the lady finished the message she was giving to a woman who was sitting on the other side of the hall to us and took a mouthful of water before she looked up and said "OK, there is a young man here. He's been waiting all evening and is extremely emotional to come through and speak." Immediately, I had the strongest and most unique feeling in my stomach, a feeling like I have never had in my entire life; I couldn't begin to know how to describe it, as it was more like a 'force within me' than a feeling as such, if that makes sense, but I knew 100% that this young man, who had been waiting patiently all evening, was Danny.

This was written up the following morning, but is the transcript of the message that was given to us......

There is a young man here, has been waiting a long time this evening. He is extremely emotional, but also very persistent to come through and speak.

He passed very recently and very, very suddenly, it was a massive shock.

He is holding the hand of a child, this child has never had an Earth life but has grown up in the spirit world, and he is holding his hand.

(It was at this point that I put up my hand and said that I thought it could be my son. The clairvoyant asked if the child was relevant and I said I didn't think so, She then asked if I had ever lost a child in miscarriage, to which I said yes, I had lost a baby 15 years ago and had always believed that it was a little boy. Steven and Becky didn't know about this, and Steven looked visibly shocked as I nodded confirmation of this fact at him. Becky, Meg and Nicole started crying.)
Our connection was made.

She said he was saying that he passed very quickly and was unaware of what was happening. It was all very confusing and wasn't in a good place as he couldn't make it out in his head. He said that there were phone calls being made.

She said, he is saying that you have a picture of him on you this evening. (*I told her about the locket I was wearing ((she was quite some distance from us))*). She said "Yes, he knows".

She suddenly said, "Wow, what a handsome boy he is! She then started laughing, adding, "Oh sorry, he is correcting me, he's saying he is not a boy, he's a man!" She added that he is 'very clued up' as well!

She asked if we were all together, as he is bouncing light around everyone on that table to indicate that lots of people are here for him tonight. He wants to say hello to everyone.

He wasn't happy about passing, but he is absolutely fine and can do anything he wants to do now.

(I was a complete mess by this point and all I could ask was "Is he OK?")

She said that spirits do not come though unless they are happy and settled in the spirit world and want to communicate with their loved ones.

She said, he doesn't like seeing you upset and struggling and that you must stay strong. He is trying to show you that he is with you all and sends messages and signs constantly, so you must listen and look out for these.

She said he is showing me a grave. She said he is shaking his finger and saying "You know you are not to associate that grave as his". She said he is happy that he wasn't put into a grave, and what you did was exactly what he would have wanted for himself and he is very happy about that.

He is saying sorry to his partner for leaving her. He didn't want to go as they didn't get enough time together to do the things they had planned and wanted to do. He wants her to go on and live a happy life and have all the happiness in the world. He just wants to see her happy.

He wants to say thank you to his brother. He can hear the prayers he has been saying for him, but don't send prayers, just talk to him normally as he can hear you. *(Steven looked quite tearful)*

She then added, "He is also telling me to say what a great time you've all had because you have just come back from

Vegas! *(I can't even begin to describe the look of shock on Steve's face - all he could say was 'Fuck me')*

And lastly, she said, "I have a bunch of flowers here and he wants me to give them to you and says you are to take them home and put them next to his picture and take his love".

To say that this evening had turned out different to how I had imagined, would be beyond an understatement. As I have said, I have always believed that we all go somewhere else when we die, and this evening had confirmed every thought I had ever had about it. Before we had come out of the hall I had glanced around at everyone else sitting in close proximity to us and literally, every one of them was in tears. As we all sat there in complete shock of the events, people were coming over and saying how beautiful it was that he had come through with a message and how tragic and emotional it was. But this was Dan…True to form, always bigger and better than everyone else! The only tiny bit of 'out of character' action was the fact that he had waited until last, and patiently … Dan was super spontaneous so waiting till last did make me wonder for a few seconds!

I took the flowers home and placed then with the picture of him that now hung on the lounge wall, from Danny's Day, just as he had asked. I got so much comfort from the message; the clairvoyant had said things that no one else could possibly have known. It had been extremely emotional and nothing was ever going to be enough to stop me aching and missing my son, but this was confirmation that he was 'OK'. It was confirmation that he was somewhere else and that he was aware of how we were all doing too. I wish I could look at as though he is on some kind of permanent holiday somewhere, but I can't. However, it is a comfort for me to believe that death isn't final and that when my time comes, whenever that may be, Danny will be waiting for me, just like his little brother was waiting for him.

When I came home and told Rich about it all, we both had a good cry about the message and the fact that our first lost baby, all those years ago, was with Dan. I know how strange and perhaps even unbelievable it may be for others to try to imagine any of this but nonetheless, we have taken great comfort in it all and after speaking to Megan and Regan about the brother that none of them ever knew, we decided from that moment that we would name that little boy after Richard's granddad, Robert and will now always refer to him as Bobby.

Signs of my Angel

It was strange that during the psychic evening, Danny had conveyed in the message that he was sending messages and signs constantly and that we were to look and listen for them. I had had a conversation with Becky only a week or so before as she pointed out that I saw signs everywhere! I agreed with her and said that there were many strange things that happened that I did believe were signs from Danny and that I took comfort in knowing he was close. The main sign that I had noticed that I got was feathers. Obviously, I didn't imagine that Dan was sitting on a cloud above me throwing these little white objects down in my direction everywhere I went! But I do believe that you are guided to walk a different way down the garden, or cross the road at a certain place, to find a feather blow across your path. I had recently been walking through a car park when noticed a feather just drifting down from the sky, there really was no bird in sight and a chap was walking towards me staring as I was looking up and walking towards him. We didn't collide but he did swerve out of my way slightly because I stopped and held my hand up, letting the feather drift into it. He just looked at me and smiled as he walked past, probably thought I was some complete nutter, but I didn't care, that feather was for me and I brought it home and placed it into a jar with all the others that have found their way to us. Upon having this conversation with Becky I said to her that maybe I do see signs everywhere, the problem is you don't, and she agreed. I said, if he is sending signs to you and you don't take any notice of them, he may stop and then what? She had thought about that but hadn't come back with anything so I just left it with her. So after the comment that was made 'to look and listen', I said that I thought that had been directed at Becky and that she was to take notice from now on. She shrugged and gave a 'yeah, maybe' expression, but it was the best I could hope for.

It wasn't just me that was seeing signs from our angel, Megan and Regan were bringing a volume of feathers home from their respective schools, but both of them finding them in corridors, under chairs or walking along the pavement! But all had blown their direction, giving cause to be seen. 'Fix you' by Coldplay seemed to be on the radio quite a lot, and considering it wasn't a new release and reduced us all to tears instantaneously, we took that as a sign. It was also quite remarkable the amount of cars that would drive past or we would see parked up with 'DAN' as part of the registration plate. Now I know Dan is not an uncommon name, but it did begin to be a bit comical seeing so many around! So other than the moulting bird population and the frequent emotion provoking music on the radio, car registration numbers were beginning to prove a more popular sign.

I had returned back to work and was now doing Wednesday and Thursday evenings and every other weekend. Although it is only a short distance to my place of work, I always drive there, pulling up outside and when finished I jump back in my car, do a U turn and arrive home less than five minutes later. One Sunday, I arrived at work to find a new lady colleague who had just started. We hit it off straightaway and spent most of the shift sharing our life stories – clearly mine was loads more interesting, emotional and unbelievable in comparison to hers and by the time my shift was done, we both felt like we had known each other years. I left and walked to my car which was parked on the road as usual, got in and did the ceremonial U turn. All of a sudden there was the most horrendous bang from under the car, as I pulled round bumping up the kerb in the usual way. The engine was still running so I thought the best thing to do was to get the car home and assess any damage then. From the sound that had been made, I thought it was bad and as I drove along the road I looked out the rear view mirror to see a river of oil following me along. An alarm started wailing and every possible light on the dashboard was flashing! I got home in record time with the engine still running and oil still pouring out of the back of the car. I telephoned Rich to tell him what had happened and after the usual "Don't worry babe, as long as you are alright, we will get it sorted" line, I looked underneath the car to see that the metal oil sump at the bottom of the engine had one hell of a large hole in it.

The next day Becky's boyfriend had a look at the car and confirmed our worries that the oil sump underneath was knackered beyond repair and that a new one would have to be fitted. This proved to be a problem as the sever knock it had taken had jammed it up against the bottom of the engine and wouldn't come off. We were told that the engine would have to come out in order to fit the new sump and that was going to be a good few hundred quid for parts and labour. As the car was thirteen years old and had an ongoing electrical fault still causing issues from the day we had got it, Rich said it would probably be better to scrap it and find a little 'run around' to get me to and from work and for shopping. On the Wednesday I went to work and my new work colleague friend was in again. I told her all about the disastrous mishap that had occurred after I had left on the Sunday and that as the damage had rendered the car un-repairable, I was sadly without wheels and needed to start looking for a new car. She mentioned that by chance, she had a friend who was selling her old car for £250. She had owned for years and was only getting rid of it because she'd recently purchased a new one; it was a little blue, 02 plate convertible and apparently, had been very well looked after. I said that I might be interested and that I would see what Rich thought and after a quick discussion, arrangements were made for Rich and me to go on the Friday to see the car.

I didn't really have the money at that precise moment to purchase a car, but as it was only £250, we decided we would find the money somehow. We drove the twenty miles or so to the address given and pulled up outside the house. There on the drive was a brand new white Mercedes and next to it was the little blue convertible. I walked up to the car and looked though the window at the interior. It all looked OK and the bodywork was in good condition considering the car was fifteen years old. It needed a good clean but I was quite excited as I had never had a convertible car before and I really did have a good feeling about it. Rich came over and began asking me what I thought about it, just as I had made my way around to the back of the car. I stood there speechless looking down at the registration number. "What's wrong, don't you like it?" He asked. I stared back at him and said "I don't care if it doesn't work at all. I am having this car, look at the letters in registration number!" Quickly moving back and tilting his head to get the same view as me and now with both of our mouths wide open, we looked at the registration of my soon to be new car.... DN ELJ

It is the most amazing sign ever and I was guided to it by my very own angel, my Daniel Jay.

I told the lady selling DN ELJ how I would love and take care of the car and told her the significance of the registration plate. She was quite overwhelmed when I gave her Danny's full name; she also stood there for a few seconds with her mouth open. She said she would charge the battery up overnight and we agreed to come back the next morning to pick it up. I was absolutely buzzing on the way home, I just couldn't stop smiling and saying to Rich "Can you believe it?" To which he kept saying he couldn't! When we got in, Rich went to collect Regan from school and I wandered down to Danny's cabin, I can't remember exactly why or if there was any specific reason or not to go in there but whilst I was pottering around, Meg's valentines card to Dan had fallen off the top of his wardrobe. I picked it up and decided to up it in a display case that he has on his wall, which contains a pair of signed boxing gloves from Anthony Joshua. As I placed the card in the case, I noticed a piece of rolled up paper at the back under one of the gloves. As I pulled it out I could see it was a folded up betting slip, with a £5.00 accumulator bet that Dan had placed at the beginning of the Premier League season in August 2016. I brought it up the house and when Rich came back I handed it to him to have a look. Dan had bet that Chelsea would win the league by a certain amount of points and that Celtic would win the Scottish Premier League. Rich took the slip and went off to the bookmakers to see if it was a winning ticket or not. He returned home some twenty minutes later with a smile on his face and said "That boy was the jammiest sod ever! He's only gone and won £350 off of a fiver!"

So thank you my darling Danny, not only did you guide me to find DN ELJ, but you also guided me to find the money to pay for it! I promise whatever happens, I will keep this car forever.

However, when we went the next morning to pick the car up and pay for it, I couldn't have been more taken aback by what the lady had to say before I drove off. She told me she was so touched to hear about how Danny had died and the connection that had brought us to buying the car, that she had done some research and knew that Danny had a memorial fund with CRY. She asked if it was OK with us if she could donate the £250 for the car, into Danny's fund. We were totally blown away by her gesture and compassion, proving that the world does have some amazingly genuine and kind people still in it.

St Georges Hospital

We arrived at St George's early morning on the 16th and spent the whole day at the hospital. Steven, Becky, Megan, Regan and I were undergoing a variety of blood tests, stress tests, symptom inducing drug tests; ECG's and ultra sound scans. During the afternoon, we had a consultation with a Professor Sharma, who after looking at all of our results, reassured us that no abnormality had shown up in any of us. Obviously this came as a massive relief, but I was disappointed that I personally hadn't shown something to be wrong, knowing that had this been the case, it would have been a confirmed indication that Danny had also carried the same faulty gene or defect, thus taking us a step further towards having something specifically accountable for the passing of my fit and healthy 25 year old son.

During our meeting, the professor told us that the worst part of his job was actually sitting with the families of a young and healthy lost loved one and giving them results of their tests. He told us that around 70% of the time that although they know it is heart related, they are unable to give an exact cause of death. Therefore, when no specific arrhythmia has been detected in the surviving family members, the cause of sudden arrhythmic death syndrome is given. They had Danny's heart, so he knew Dan didn't have heart disease or deterioration and as most of these fatal arrhythmias are undetectable after death, so to have an exact diagnosis in these circumstances would be extremely rare. The professor then proceeded to ask me if I had any questions and what I knew of a condition called Brugada, adding that he was now aware that Danny did have Brugada syndrome and that this is what caused his heart to stop whilst he was asleep. He said that the test done and subsequent results showing that none of us were affected by this condition meant that it would be classed as 'sporadic' to Danny, starting with him, rather than being hereditary. This information was coming from nowhere at us and I couldn't take in what he was saying at first. I started to cry, quickly looking round at the others, sitting beside me, for their reaction to this news. I said that if this condition was undetectable after death, how was he so sure? I added that I had noticed on Danny's post mortem report that an ECG taken in July 2009 mentioned a 'part bundle branch block'. I said to the professor that I didn't understand what that was and that reading the post mortem report was the first time I had been aware of it and knew for certain that Danny had never known he had it. To the horror of all of us sitting there, we watched as the professor pulled an ECG from Danny's file. He handed it to me and said "We only managed to obtain this last week. This is a copy of the ECG that was taken in July 2009. Looking at it clearly shows that Daniel (then aged 17) had a definitive Right Bundle Branch Block and also at the time the tracing was taken, registered what we as cardiologists class as a high risk Brugada pattern".

Here and totally unprepared, I was being given the answer to the question I had longed for since the day he had died, but never thought I would get. Here in my hands, in black and white was the reason Danny had died. All those years there had been something wrong with my perfectly healthy child and not one of us had known anything about it. After five months of knowing absolutely nothing about his sudden and tragically premature death, the cause was Brugada Syndrome. I sat there shaking and crying uncontrollably, while trying to take it all in. I just stared at that A4 piece of grey paper with the tracing of Danny's heartbeat etched across it and Daniel Brown faintly printed in the top left hand corner. I felt sick for believing that if I actually had the cause to blame for his death, it would help me understand or accept it a little easier. But this didn't help, this shocking revelation made it much, much worse. I never imagined anything in life could be more devastating than finding my child dead but this was. This was becoming more horrendously shocking and on so many different levels, than any of us sitting in that room were prepared for. We were suddenly being told by the Professor that Danny actually had two heart conditions, both of which had been detected eight years before his death and that our own GP, who had looked at these ECG results at the time, had noted an abnormality onto Dan's medical records, but had failed to ever inform us that a defect had be found. He said that although Brugada syndrome is incurable, it is treatable and sudden death is preventable.

It had taken over five months since Danny had passed away for us to finally have a specific cause for his death but unfortunately, that in itself brought us very little comfort. I looked at Steve and Becky sitting there, both of them trying to absorb what he had just said. Megan and Regan were crying but did not really understand the magnitude that these undisclosed ECG results had played in Dan's sudden death. Professor Sharma began to gently explain that Danny would have known nothing about it at all; he said it is literally 'lights out'; he would have felt nothing, just fell asleep and peacefully drifted away. Now it's a known certainty, as we all live, we all eventually die and here we were being told that Danny had died the best possible way, in a way that I would want, not only for myself, but for all those I love, when their time comes. Dan wasn't ill, so there had been no suffering, he wasn't involved in an accident, so he hadn't experienced any pain and he wasn't maliciously hurt by anyone, so he would have felt no fear. Looking at Danny's death in that way allows me to understand that everyone dies for a reason and that was his. Although he was far too young, he had always lived an amazingly happy and fulfilled life and that is something that is denied to many.

I have always believed in fate and destiny and truly thought that as time progressed, I would come to accept that this was Danny's time, his fate, his destiny. But knowing what I know now, that for over eight years our own GP surgery had been aware of his heart defect and had failed to inform him. It was blatantly obvious that although we had been given the actual cause of his death as Brugada Syndrome, we were also now vividly aware that 'someone' was also accountable for this tragedy. This should never have happened, this was not his time, his fate or destiny, this was medical negligence from our own GP and that is something I will never be able to accept, EVER.

The Medical Records

As soon as we arrived home from St Georges, I telephoned our GP surgery and requested an appointment with one of the practice managers. This was arranged for 16th October 2017. Although it was four weeks away, I wanted them to be prepared and have every document and record that was relevant to Danny available when I went in. As Danny had now been gone for over five months, his medical records had been closed and sent away for archiving, so the surgery needed to get them back because I wanted to see them, not just those relating to chest and back pains that he had incurred over the years, which they had always said were 'growing pains' or 'musculoskeletal', I wanted access to his full medical records, dating back from his birth.

I attended the appointment in the evening of Monday 16th October with my brother, Dean. I knew that I would be a complete mess and although Richard said he would come with me, I needed someone who was more emotionally together and would be able to take on board all that would be discussed. Dean was amazing; I started crying from the moment I walked into the surgery as Danny's medical records popped up on the screen in red with the word DECEASED written above his name. Somehow they had also put the wrong date of death on his records and when I pointed this out, the GP was mortified and very apologetic. The whole meeting was an astounding revelation. We scrutinised every visit Danny had made to the surgery for over a decade and it showed a catalogue of errors and missed opportunities. When we eventually got to see the actual July 2009 ECG that Danny had given in the surgery, it clearly showed that the referring GP had written on in RBBB (Right Bundle Branch Block). He had also written a comment onto Dan's medical notes.... *Action referral letter to Cardiologist for further investigation.* This referral had never been sent. This had been Danny's window of opportunity and they had failed to open it for him. Reading that little sentence on his notes completely blew what was left of my world apart. Danny had died un-necessarily because of a clerical error failing to send him to see a cardiologist. I was beyond stunned and sat in complete silence while Dean took up the reigns and started barraging the doctor with questions. Looking on further from the date of that ECG, the records showed that between 2011 and ironically, 9th March 2015 being the last, Danny made eleven visits to the surgery because of upper back or chest pain. Each time a trivial reason was given and not one of those GP's, that Dan presented his concerns too, looked back through his medical notes, referred to the ECG or showed enough concern for his reoccurring chest discomfort to investigate it further. Not one of them had informed him of his RBBB, probably because they didn't know themselves because they hadn't read his notes. But most tragically, their attitude to the fact that he was a young, fit and otherwise healthy and sporty young man who didn't show any 'text book' heart problem symptoms, assisted them all in their failure to notice that the cardiology referral that could have saved his life, had never actually been done.

We left the surgery after about an hour or so, after the GP had agreed to get copies of all Danny's medical history for us to keep. This was going to take a few days and then he said a thorough investigation would take place to find out exactly what had gone so terribly wrong. None of this was going to make the slightest piece of difference, it was never going to bring Danny back and it was certainly never going to make me accept that Dan would have died in the same way had he been given his chance to be diagnosed, monitored and treated eight years ago. Dean and I sat in his car, in the practice car park, as I cried myself into numbness. He hugged me as we sat in silence for a few minutes before the quietness was broken by him saying 'Oh Shelly, I am so sorry, what a complete fuck up, poor Danny'. It was a complete fuck up, it was a waste of his beautiful young life, it was un-necessary and beyond tragic. I had truly believed that nothing could get any worse, but yet again, I was wrong because this was the lowest point I had ever reached. I had fallen to the ultimate bottom of hell, all those times Dan had known something wasn't right and they had sat there with the answer staring them in the face all the time. They had done nothing other than deny my son countless chances to live a long and relatively normal life, but now everything was too late. I was heartbroken and angrier than I had ever been in my entire life, what a needless and tragic waste of such a young and perfect life.

I obtained the medical records for Dan a few weeks later and brought them home to study in great detail. A few weeks passed before I basically had mustered up enough emotional and mental strength to write a letter to the surgery. I had spoken with a solicitor, not for anything other than advice on how to approach this minefield of negligence. The solicitor asked me what I hoped to achieve from going down this path. I told him that all I wanted was an apology. I didn't want to pursue any kind of financial claim and although in my head, I could hear Danny screaming at me to take the bastards for every penny they have, this was not going to bring him back. No amount of money would ever change how we coped with Dan's loss and I wasn't about to put a price on his life. I wanted them to be sorry and admit and accept that his heath was most definitely their fault. The solicitor said it was highly unlikely that we would ever get an apology and that if legal representation got involved, it could take years to get anywhere because the GP surgery would then have to step back and pass any direct correspondence relating to Danny's care, or lack of it, onto their own legal team. He advised me to write a letter as a mother, asking for answers and see how far we could get keeping it personal between me and the surgery. So that is what I decided to do. I wanted answers and an apology for Danny and so I wrote to them....

Dear Sir,   *24th November 2017*

I find it necessary to write this most difficult of letter to you in relation to my son, Daniel.

Danny was perfectly fit and healthy when he tragically passed away in his sleep in the early hours of March 9th 2017. I don't know if you are a parent, but I truly believe nothing would ever be more devastating and heartbreaking than to find your 25 year old child dead in their bed. Danny's sudden passing in this way with no illness, accident, reason or explanation attributing to it has had our family endure a suffering of grief and shock of the worst kind possible and on a level unimaginable. Being told that he had just 'died in his sleep' had horrendous consequences on me, both physically and mentally for months after he died. It's hard enough to just function from day to day, but being unable to sleep for any length of time without medication, made life unbearable. I became paranoid, spending most of the night wandering into the bedrooms of my other children to check that they were still breathing. Danny leaves four other siblings, the youngest being a brother of 10 and sister age 12, who to this day still cannot accept or understand how we all sat having dinner the evening before to come home from school and be told their brother had died. Due to the sudden and unexplained nature surrounding Danny's death, we were told by the coroner that his heart had to be being sent to St Georges Hospital in Tooting for further investigations. At this time, his post mortem had concluded a cause of death as 'unknown', stating that every organ in his body was structurally normal and healthy. The coroner said that investigations could take months and unfortunately they would not be able to issue us with a death certificate or release him to us for a funeral to take place, if we wanted his heart to be reunited with him. This was another devastating decision to make, but I found myself having no choice in the matter than to agree to these conditions. Danny's heart was permanently removed and we were able to make plans and lay him to rest three and a half weeks later, without a death certificate.

My son's post-mortem report came back to us towards the end of May, the cause of death stated as 'Sudden Arrhythmic Death Syndrome'. I read Danny's post-mortem report and can honestly say that for the rest of my life I will wish that I hadn't. No parent would ever want to associate their child alongside such brutally descriptive comments of what is undertaken during this procedure, but he is my son and once read, can't be un-read. However, it was this report that first made me aware that Danny had a 'part bundle branch block', a heart defect that neither he nor myself had ever been made aware of, so I assumed that this had been discovered during his PM.

As Danny was part of a large family and because his death certificate indicated the cause as being related to his heart, we all had to spend a day at St Georges Inherited Cardiac Clinic in London for screening. Danny's four siblings, his Dad and I underwent lots of test to detect whether any of us had any kind of heart defect. The hospital was specifically looking for one which could determine for certain as to whether Danny had died of a condition known as Brugada Syndrome. This life threatening arrhythmia can affect those with a structurally normal and healthy heart. It is not detectable after death and diagnosis is made either through a sufferer giving a positive ECG reading or by changes to the rhythm of the heart when administering a drug called Ajmaline. Thankfully, the outcome of all tests for the rest of the family resulted in 'the all clear' being given. We had to wait and see the head cardiologist at St Georges to discuss, not only our results but also the hospitals findings on tests that they had carried out on Danny's heart.

Professor Sharma asked me if I had any questions about Danny's tragic death and what I knew about Brugada Syndrome. I instantly asked about the post mortem reference to the 'part bundle branch block' and what side of the heart it had affected and whether this was relevant to his death. He turned to a file on his desk that he had on my son and pulled out a copy of an ECG he had obtained from our GP surgery the week prior to our visit. His response was beyond shocking and something none of us sitting there were prepared for. He's exact words were, "It was a right bundle branch block and we are now certain that Daniel died of Brugada Syndrome". We were horrified by this and I was extremely emotional saying it was my understanding that Brugada was not detectable after death and as the tests had shown none of us had Brugada, how were they so sure Danny did? Holding up the piece of paper he added, "This ECG was taken in July 2009 and although it is a bad copy, it clearly shows that Daniel had a RBBB, which someone has written on the reading itself. More importantly though, it also shows a tracing of a high risk Brugada pattern and this is what confirms a definitive diagnosis that Danny had it".

In light of this devastating revelation, I contacted the surgery at the beginning of September and spoke with a GP. He kindly told me that although it could take a few weeks, he would get all of Danny's historic medical records together and as soon as this was done, he would call me in so we could discuss everything. I attended this meeting with my brother and the GP on 16th October.

I have always been a rather 'over-protective' mum to each one of my five children, especially in relation to their health. Other than obvious visual symptoms to illnesses and injuries, I have no medical training or ability to diagnose any underlying conditions, except of course a mother's gut instinct in knowing that something isn't right. It is because of my lack of medical knowledge and when a child of mine has come to me saying they feel unwell, I have entrusted the wellbeing of those most precious people in my life into the hands of "professionals". During our meeting with the doctor, we spent an hour looking through Danny's records and isolating the visits for just chest and back pain that he had presented to various GP's, the first one being on 24/3/04 until the last, which ironically was 9/3/15. It quickly became apparent *that every single GP who 'treated' my son appears to have failed in reviewing the consultation notes of any previous visits he had made. Not one of them checked his records, his ECG results or was concerned enough by his symptoms to show that tests and recommendations for further investigation were ever acted upon. I find it inconceivable in understanding how this was a reoccurring chest problem for years and therefore possibly related to his heart, would not have prompted at least one of the GP's to delve further into actually getting a cardiologists opinion? Catastrophically for Danny, the life threatening information which was recorded on that ECG performed in your surgery on 1st July 2009 under the instructions of another GP, was never put in the summary notes section of his medical records. Unbelievably, another missed opportunity for this vital information to be included somewhere prominent on his records was following a visit he made on 24/7/09, where copies of the records show another Doctor requested a referral to a cardiologist. This referral was never done. Tragically, these were Danny's most obvious 'windows of opportunity' and they were all missed.*

When I questioned as to whether a RBBB was not an important enough condition to be on the summary notes section of his records, the GP told us a diagnosis of an RBBB should definitely have been included in this section of the medical records. He added that this is what GP's refer to minutes prior to an appointment with a patient. It enables them to 'familiarise' themselves with any acute or chronic conditions the patient has. It allows a GP to look back over the last four or five visits that a patient has made regarding a specific condition. However, the records you held on Danny prove that this was not the case, as he's lacked the vital information being noted where it should have been.

I have chronologically listed all the times from 2004 to 2015 that your surgery dealt with chest and back pain consultations, tests, treatment or even just recording the results in relation to Danny. There are 18 individual noted occasions. I completely fail to see how whether a simple clerical error or a GP oversight for whatever reason, was constantly overlooked. This negligence contributes to a monumental catalogue of errors from the surgery and resulted in failure to ensure that my 25 year old child received the proper medical care when he needed it. For over eight years he was denied the chance, the choice and countless missed opportunities, not only be told that there was actually something wrong, but in allowing him to be diagnosed, monitored and therefore treated for this condition. It is a fact that once diagnosed, Brugada sufferers can live a normal life and sudden death can be prevented. Tragically for Danny, his family, his fiancé and his friends, he was not given that choice or those chances or any other opportunity to take a different path in life and because of that he has died and we all have to live with the consequences of that every day.

I never imagined that anything could actually be worse than finding my child dead, but knowing that this was detected over eight years ago and had a proper duty of care been provided to Danny, he would still be here with us today. This tragedy could have been so easily prevented, but for us all left merely existing and knowing this, does actually make this nightmare so much worse.

I would appreciate if someone could look into this for me. This was Danny's life and that life is now over. I know nothing is going to bring him back and that nothing can change the way we all have to learn to live for the rest of our lives without him. Nothing will help us accept his death or our understanding of the circumstances that surrounded it and have placed us where we find ourselves today. Nothing can help ease our grief. I always knew that there had to be a reason to why Danny had died. There is a reason behind every death and something was responsible for his. Now sadly over seven months later and after seeing his medical records and speaking with a GP at the surgery, it is quite clear that your practice is accountable for Danny's sudden and premature death at the age of 25, because of undiagnosed Brugada Syndrome. Should you find that the professional conduct throughout all of this differs in any way from that normally followed at the practice, or what you would expect from your staff, taking into consideration the amount of times my son came to you for help and the opportunities that were missed, I would be most grateful for your opinion or at least an explanation regarding his treatment, or lack of it. I believe the practice has shown gross negligence towards Danny and ask that should any findings through your investigation agree with me, I would like to make it clear, that all we ask from the practice as a devastated family is an apology for him. I really don't feel this is too great a request under the circumstances, as the difference any apology will make to our lives would be minimal. I only hope that following an investigation and an admission of failure towards him would ensure that the name Daniel Brown is never forgotten at that surgery. I hope that acknowledging such a monumental oversight, which has attributed to the most tragic of consequences for a young man with such a promising life ahead of him, will never be repeated at your surgery. I have included some pictures of Danny so you can actually put a face to the kindest and most beautiful son, brother and fiancé whose amazing life, is now over.

I await your response.

After a week or so I heard back from the surgery, acknowledging receipt of my letter and that an investigation would be taking place but due to the complexity of the case, it could take some amount of time to get hold of GP's that no longer worked at the surgery and collate information together enabling my questions to be answered and concerns to be addressed. I wasn't going anywhere; nothing was going to change any of this now, so I just sat tight and waited to hear from them again. Christmas 2017 came and went and I still hadn't heard anything back. It was the beginning of March and we were doing a Memorial Golf Day and fundraising evening to mark Danny's 26th birthday. The snow came, so the golf itself was postponed until May, but the fundraising event went ahead. Because everything was a bit manic, I had decided to hold out on contacting the surgery until after the event, but I had been getting more infuriated by their lack of contact with each passing week, so on the 1st anniversary of Danny's passing and literally at the end of my tether, I wrote yet another letter….

Dear Sir   *9th March 2018*

I write to you in relation to a letter sent to you regarding my son, Daniel Brown, on 24th November 2017.

I did receive an acknowledgement of receipt from you shortly afterwards and subsequently a follow up letter just before Christmas, stating that due to the complexity of the matter, it would take longer than originally expected to investigate.

I can appreciate that some doctors who once worked at your practice have left, but I cannot understand why it's taking so long or actually why you need to contact them for an opinion? I find it unlikely to imagine they would remember what was discussed during a consultation with my son after such a long period of time. I don't understand why you don't look back through the documentation that you have on Danny. This is recorded, written clarification of a handful of GP's and their varying reactions and written request of actions to be take, in relation to the many chest pain visits that Danny had made to them at surgery over the period of nine years?

Today marks one year since I walked in to the room of my 25 year old, fit and healthy son and found he had passed away in his sleep. Danny died not knowing he had Brugada Syndrome. He died not knowing that he also had a right bundle branch block. Danny died never knowing that there was actually something wrong with his heart. He always knew something wasn't right due to the reoccurring pain he suffered which caused him to make so many visits to GP's at the surgery for help. Nothing is ever going to change the situation we as a family are in, nor will it ease the pain of complete devastation that we live with every day. The issue here is that your surgery did know something was wrong, you knew he had a right bundle branch block because it was recorded on the ECG that was taken in the surgery in July 2009, it also recorded that his heart rhythm was not normal (a doctor told us in October 2017 that although he wouldn't have known it was Brugada, he would have recognised it as not being a normal rhythm). The doctor who recorded this life threatening information from the ECG, wrote on Danny's medical records that he be seen by a Cardiologist for further investigation.

Now I am not familiar with how long it actually takes to investigate a medical negligence error and guess that if a patient's records are hard to come by, then this could take a considerable amount of time. But this is not the case here and I am starting to feel that the chance of getting an apology from you for Danny is slowly ebbing away. You have documentation to hand (as do I), which shows your lack of professionalism in informing Danny of his abnormal ECG results, plus the catastrophic error in failing to refer him to a cardiologist all those years ago. It is written in black and white that the practice prevented Danny and his family from being aware that something was wrong, giving us a chance to seek professional advice on lifestyle changes that could possibly exacerbate the condition, the chance of him having frequent monitoring for changes in severity of reoccurring symptoms and the choice of various available treatments. But tragically, and the hardest thing that we have to live with now, is knowing he was denied the opportunity to be fitted with a defibrillator which would have prevented his premature and un-necessary death at 25 years of age.

I am not looking for any individual to point the finger of blame at. I knew something was responsible for Danny's death and after months and family testing we were told exactly what that was. However, what I wasn't prepared for was that 'someone'' was accountable for knowing something was wrong, yet not informing us in a time where it would have made a difference to Danny still being alive today. In my opinion, this is where the responsibility in a duty of care falls at your door and that the least we deserve and Danny certainly deserves through having his life cut short at the age of 25, is a 'sorry'.

I await your response.

Thankfully and on March 26th 2018, I received a response from the surgery. Although they never directly stated in their very long letter that they were directly responsible for Danny's death or admitted liability in their failings towards him on the multiple occasions that he went to them, they did apologise for the pain and suffering that we as a family now endured. They acknowledged that that they had recognised many areas where their systems and procedures required substantial improvement and that a cardiologist would be brought into the practice to advise all GP's working there, how to recognise the many abnormal arrhythmias on ECG readings, especially those in relation to Brugada syndrome. I had a personal letter included with the surgery one, from the doctor who wrote 'refer to cardiologist' on Dan's medical records. It was a difficult letter to read, he apologised unreservedly for the distress that has been caused. He went on to add that he 'lives with the deepest regret' if his failure in requesting the referral at the end of the day, contributed to our loss.

There are many changes being made at the surgery and they have asked for my direct input in sitting with them and help with the wording and planning of leaflets advising patients of acceptable waiting times to hear back from referrals. The referrals themselves will now be done whilst the patient is sitting with the GP and not left until the surgery closes. They will no longer perform ECG's in the surgery, instead patients will be sent to the local hospital where a cardiologist will record the findings accurately, before notifying and passing them on to the practice. They have promised me that many lessons have been learned and they are deeply sorry for the distress that has been caused by Danny's tragic death. They said that Daniel Brown will never be forgotten at the practice and that because of their change of approach in how they will now deal with referrals, they will be putting up posters in prominent locations around the practice.

I may not have got a 'sorry' for Danny or a written admission of guilt at the negligence that was clearly bestowed upon him, but all the changes that have and are being made at there now, are enough to prove to me and everyone else, that they know they are responsible for his premature death. Clearly if they didn't think they were in the wrong, they wouldn't make any changes at all.
I have gone as far as I can with this. I have dotted the I's and crossed the T's, just like I promised Dan I would, it is another tragically lose end that has now been tied up. If in the coming years, the changes made at the practice and in their approach to patients, spares one family the heartache that we live with everyday through a life being saved, then that will be because of Danny, and that really has to be a good enough legacy.

All of the changes being made at the surgery bring me no comfort at all. I am stuck between a rock and a hard place, faced with the dilemma of do I look for another doctor's surgery for my family, out of loyalty to Danny because of how he was treated? Or do we stay at the surgery, with the potential lifetime guarantee that because of their massively tragic failings towards him, they will never let another one of my children down so horrifically. Is it better the devil you know or not? I am at a loss. I try to think what Danny would say, I know he'd be beyond mad about it all, but knowing the person he was, he'd probably say that his siblings were better off staying put, because those GP's wouldn't dare to make such a monumental fuck up to our family ever again. I have had so many people say to me how great it is that they have accepted their failings and are making such dynamic changes and yes it is, but why did it take so long, why does all this have to happen now and why did it have to be because of my son. It is just so devastatingly sad and I feel forever exhausted by the constant thought of all that has happened. It is inconceivable that the simplest of actions were overlooked and have resulted in the direst of consequences for Danny. I shall never be able to accept or come to terms with any of this and something I can't move away from; it really is just the worst it can possibly be.

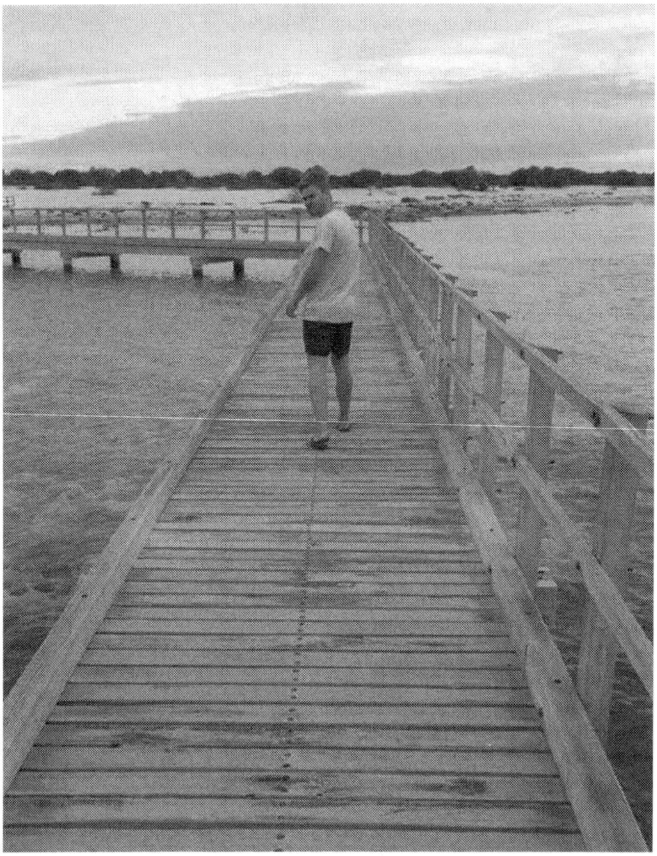

A life without Dan

Every day is different. Some day's I go through them relatively normal, yet others are such a struggle. It is the most stupid things that prompt an emotional eruption and usually occur when I am not even thinking about Dan. I may be doing the washing up, putting shopping away or picking up the kids dirty clothes in their rooms when 'BAM', no gradual build up or warning anymore, it instantly hits like I've been stabbed in the middle of my chest, a surge of emotion and pain which causes me to burst into tears as reality screams in my face once again, that Danny has gone, my beautiful son has gone forever and bloody hell, it really does hurt. The fact that these unpredictable emotional outburst can happen at any time have had a massive impact on everything I do. I am not comfortable going out with friends or even spending time in the company of others, just because of the uncertainty of how I will be from one moment to the next. Friends were there in the first few months after Danny passed, but I couldn't cope with the 'normality' of going out for lunch or spending an evening or afternoon in someone else's home like I did before we had lost him. They were trying the best they could and the only way they really knew how, so if we were invited out, we went but inside felt constantly uncomfortable, a bit like the 'ducks on a pond' expression, calm on the surface but paddling frantically underneath.

Sadly, life does move on and I struggled and failed to keep up as everything around us started to revert back to being the same. For us, nothing was the same anymore and after about eight months, I felt that friends and some family members had literally thrown the ball of control into my court and took a step back. I was told all the time "if you need me, give me a call", the problem was that I didn't need anyone around me in those first few months; I was just existing and drifting along. What I needed was for my close friends, and even some family members, to understand and be there for us in those difficult months that lay ahead. I quickly became aware that the only place I felt comfortable was being at home. I didn't have it in me to call round uninvited to people's houses, or ask them if they fancied a lunch out with this sad bereaved mum and therefore, the only time spent in the company of others was if I took my Mum to a hospital appointment or received the very occasional text asking if I fancied meeting up for a lunch. I literally spent day after day and week after week just hoping for a knock at the door and see a familiar face standing there saying, "I can't stay long, just popped round to see how you are" or "I don't care if you're not dressed, put the kettle on I've only got ten minutes!" But no one called and I slowly realised that this is how life was now going to be from now on.

I had returned back to work within two months of Danny's death and my part time hours were adjusted to accommodate Rich and me working around Megan and Regan. We no longer had the luxury of Danny being at home to sit with them for a couple of hours when our shifts overlapped. It is strange when I look back as at the time of writing this, it has been over fifteen months since Dan passed away and yet it only seems like a few weeks since I last saw him, held him and had a conversation with him. So much has happened and yet my recollection of anything unassociated directly with Danny throughout this period of time is very vague. Everything around us has gone back to being the same as it was before he died, but as a family everything is different because nothing will ever be the same without him.

I hope that anyone reading this book never finds themselves in my situation. It is a book that I certainly will wish everyday for the rest of my life that I never had been given reason to write. I cannot give advice to anyone on how to deal with the death of a child. Everyone's grief is different because every parent's attachment to their child will differ. Grief is a unique and personal journey, a lifelong journey of learning how to carry the pain of real heartbreak alongside you. Some days it is so heavy, you have no choice other than to stop and just accept that you cannot continue at that moment and yet other days, it is more bearable. I never intended to write a book, this all started as sporadic moments in a diary, or what my counsellor referred to as grief journal. I found it easier to write down all the emotions I was experiencing that I couldn't physically express out loud. It is not easy to explain a feeling which is so deeply painful and raw. Through constantly adding paragraphs of everything that has happened, I have found it has put this horrific nightmare into some sort of order. This is how I remember it and this may very well differ to the recollection of the rest of the family who were so directly involved in it from the very beginning. I started writing it as a book seven months after losing Danny during October 2017 and today, as I write this sentence on Thursday 9th

August 2018, Dan has been gone from our lives for exactly 74 weeks.

Although we are still in the very early stages of living without Dan, the shock is still a constant companion and continues to take my breath and makes my heart sink as the reality returns, if I have being doing something and his loss momentarily strays from the forefront of my mind. My view on live is unrecognisable to what it was, I don't look forward to anything, there is no excitement anymore. I don't know if in time that will return and to be brutally honest, I don't care if it doesn't, Danny will always be missing from my life and without him I am incomplete as a mum. I had a conversation with Steven a couple of weeks back and made a promise to him and myself, one which I will not break, regardless of how this journey pans out for us all. I said to him that although I am not the wife, the daughter, sister or friend that I was, I will channel every ounce of my soul into once again being the mum that I was to all five of my children, the mum I was when Danny was here. I feel I owe it to Danny's memory and to the needs of Steve, Becky, Megan and Regan to be the Mum I was. The mum they could always come to with their problems, any advice they needed or just for a chat and a shoulder to cry upon. I will not allow Danny's death to make me a different mum to the one he always came to. But most importantly, I don't want his siblings looking back on life in years to come and seeing me as a mum that became unrecognisable after they lost their brother. Life was perfect and now it can never be that way again and as a family, we all accept that. Like it or not, we have to carry on and learn to make the best of what we have, Dan was no more important or loved more than his brothers and sisters and I will never want them to ever feel like he was. He is just missed so, so much more.

The only piece of advice I would offer to those who have never lost a child would be to think very carefully before you offer platitudes or comforting words to a bereaved parent. No loss is greater than losing a child and no other kind of loss that you may have experienced can be compared to it. You cannot, and hopefully never will, be able to begin to imagine or understand the living hell that parent is enduring on a daily basis. I cannot recall how many times people have said to me, "Oh you are so strong and inspirational", or "I just couldn't carry on if it had happened to me". Well you don't really have that much of a choice! I want to curl up and die myself most days, but I have four other children struggling to deal with the loss of their brother, so you have to get a grip as often as is possible, just to "be strong and inspirational" for them, when all you really wish for, is to be that person that you once were, before this horrendous event destroyed you and your family.

Remember, it really doesn't matter how sincere and genuine you are, you will never be able say the right thing, only the wrong! There are no words of comfort that exist which will make bereaved mums or dads feel better. There are no positives to be taken from such a devastating and life changing event, so don't try to offer any. Never say the ,'Give it time' or 'It's still early days' line, no amount of time is going to make the loss any easier to bare. You don't stop loving that child any less as time goes on, but you sure as hell miss them and long for them more and more with each passing day. I think people only say something because they feel they should, when really, they shouldn't because they just don't understand. So don't try to 'cheer' us up, don't try to 'take our mind off things' and don't give us examples of your experiences with grief, if you have any. You cannot help us with our pain or our loss and with the best intentions in the world; you certainly cannot take it away from us. I think the best thing you can give to anyone who has lost their child is a hug and the offer of a shoulder to cry on. Sometimes we don't want to speak, we just want to cry, we don't need you to try and understand, we just want to be held and yes, sometimes we will talk about the excruciating pain within us and for you to acknowledge that we are hurting so unimaginably and hopefully just support us until it stops, because nothing makes any sense to us and it never will.

The one final thing is never under estimate that death changes absolutely everything. The loss of that child has changed the lives of those surviving individuals forever. They are no longer the wife, the husband, the son, daughter, sister, brother or friend that they were and will probably never look at life in the way that they did before. So from personal experience, I shall give one simple, piece of advice to those of you who may find yourselves looking into our world from the outside.... Give us time, it's still early days, stand alongside us and help support us with our grief and our absentmindedness, our occasional dismissive attitude or uninterested approach to your way of life. You may sometimes see a small flicker of that once fun loving, carefree and loyal person or maybe you won't, but hopefully some of you, if not most, will learn to live and love the different friend or family member that through no choice of our own, we have now become. You may long for that person to return, just as we too will spend the rest of our lives longing to be that person and have the perfect life and complete family that we once had.

Memories of Others

It was never my intention to write a book, it originally started as a grief journal. At the beginning, I never imagined that by writing down every painful second, remembering every shallow breath and crippling step that I took after losing my beautiful son, I would be able to piece together an organised timeline of everything. In those first few days, all I had was a million constantly destructive thoughts crashing about in my head. There was no light at the end of the tunnel. I was never in a tunnel. I was in the darkest hole and there was nowhere to run and no one to help get me away from the reality of what was happening. I have found solace in writing and putting things into an order which has helped me see them more clearly. I have been able to lift some of the pain from within my heart, which I couldn't verbally say but found easier to put onto paper. It is truly the most painful journey anyone could make and for those of us who loved Danny, it will last a lifetime. I shall never get over the shock of those first few seconds when I found Dan, it still hits me like a punch in the stomach when I think about it. Nor shall I ever accept the failings of the GP surgery, who if had been through in their treatment of Danny all those years ago, would have allowed him to still be here today, living his life to the full, having holidays and making plans, who knows, maybe even setting a date for his and Meg's wedding and I would never have had any reason to write this book.

But this chapter is not about my opinion, my thoughts, memories or description of Danny. This chapter is called

Memories of Others and that is exactly what it is. Danny had so many friends and I have asked those who wanted to contribute, to share a memory that they have of him for this book. This book is about Danny and to anyone who may read it, should know by now exactly how much I love him and what he meant to me! This chapter will hopefully show you that I wasn't being biased. Danny was deeply loved and what with his spontaneous and fun loving attitude, his kind and caring manner and his magnetic and quick witted personality, he created many a great time with others and was centre of many a memorable occasions, not just for friends and family but anyone who was blessed to have been in his company.

I will forever be immensely proud of my son and it gives me the greatest pleasure to share with you, just a few moments of what others thought of the real Danny Brown.....

I am Danny's big brother, Steven. I have countless memories of good times, bad times, laughs and fights that Dan and I shared, which start as far back as I can remember and go right up until the last time I ever saw him, when he dropped me off at our Dad's house after the West Ham v Chelsea game on the Monday night, just before driving off, he asked me to run in and grab his hair gel he'd left behind after his birthday party. Being only 13 months older than Dan, I don't remember anything in my life before he arrived. Although we were complete opposites in our approach to life, me being more cautious and methodical, compared to Dan who had to be first to do something, always jumped in with both feet and would only worry about any consequences if they occurred! Apart from those obvious differences, we were still so alike in many other ways. Dan was my first friend, my allied partner in crime and my best mate. I miss my brother and think of him all the time. Even at the time of writing these few memories, it's been 18 months since he died and I still cannot actually believe he has gone. It feels unreal.

Dan and I used to play footie in dining room in old house. I used to go in goal and he would shoot at me with a sponge ball. The goal frame was the dining room table legs and top of it was the cross bar! We used to play up to number 20, with each goalkeeper getting better after each goal. For some reason that I can't recall, number 7 used to be the tough goalie and not number 20 as you'd think! Mum and Dad had this expensive crystal temperature gauge ornament which had been brought back from Germany, this sat some distance away from the goal posts on the dining room. This one time however, Dan took a shot and the ball rebounded off something, either me or the dining table, up and over the large and bulky Tiny PC, rolling along the shelf and dropped onto the mantel piece where this crystal ornament stood. The ball hit the

ornament softly but was enough to knock it over! With both of us watching with shocked facial expressions, we temporarily thought we were safe until the ornament start to roll towards the edge. There was nothing either of us could do to stop the inevitable from happening and we watched as the ornament fell from the mantel piece onto the wooden floor, smashing into a thousand pieces. We looked at each other and knew we were in big trouble. Although, so many years on, I don't really remember the telling off we would have got, I will never forget that silly football game we both loved to play in the dining room. Steve x

---

Just after returning from Malia in 2012 Dan asked me if I wanted to go with him to West Ham's first game of the season as against Aston Villa Grant couldn't go if I remember right. Even though I'm an Arsenal fan Dan always knew I'd happily go to any game of football.

The game was boring as anything and my only entertainment came from Dan's moaning! But one highlight was the weather. I can honestly say it was one of the nicest summer days I can ever remember in England. It was boiling hot not a cloud in the sky and at half time me and Dan started talking about the possibility of going V festival the next day, with Dan especially keen.

There had been no talk of going this year as we had camped there the previous two years and thought our time there was done. But after just coming back from Malia a few days previously we was still in that holiday mood and with the weather like this we thought we could at least see if there were any tickets online.

We got the train back home and Dan said he'd let me know what he found, he was always good at looking up things online and getting deals. At around 9pm I hadn't heard from Dan and accepted we probably wasn't going. Soon after I get a text from Dan saying he's found two tickets on eBay and the seller is from...Elm Park!

We was proper laughing, you couldn't make it up. So we walked up to Elm Park together at about half 10 at night to meet the seller. We end up knocking on the wrong door where some old boy started looking out his curtains thinking we was there to burgle his house! Luckily the next door neighbour came out and we got the tickets.

Off we went the next day just us two and we got a train to Chelmsford. We stopped off at Tesco at about 11am and bought a bottle of white wine each, classy as ever. We mixed the wine with lemonade to not look like total alcoholics and headed to the festival. When we arrived we was already on our way and to be honest we probably peaked too early! But I remember me and Dan just laughing at anything and everything and both being in tears of laughter throughout the day.

In previous years at V we went in large groups and it was always a case of following each other round so we could all see the acts we wanted to see. This was always good but with me and Dan just there on our own we decided we didn't want to be rushing around and just had a good old laugh and a good drink up. I can't even remember the acts we saw, most of the day we was just laying on the grass with a drink in our hands enjoying the sun and laughing at some of the strange sights you usually see at a festival.

We even had a kip while Tom Jones was on and were only woken up by the rain. In a drunken state and in a panic to stop rain going in our beers we covered the cups with our phones...not our best moment! We sobered up just in times for the Killers and what an end to the day and me and Dan both said it was one of the best live acts we'd seen.

I can honestly say that day with Dan was my best time at V festival. The times we went as groups were brilliant, but the laughs me and Dan had that day could not be topped and Dan always said the same. Two lads going to a festival on their own might not be the most normal thing to some, but I couldn't think of a better person to have been with that day. Jack.

A memory I've just remembered was when me, James and Dan were at Romford dogs about 1 year ago. Dan loved doing a tricksy but rarely won. This evening he placed a tricast on a race and came back absolutely fuming because the woman had put the wrong number down on it! Anyway, Dan decided to leave it as what had been given, the race finished and the cheeky sod only ended up winning £100! Always so lucky!   Grant.

Danny,

You where always late back from your lunch break so, I lent you a bike so you would have more time.

It made no difference because you were still late back, but you just had more time at home eating you Mums yummy spaghetti bolognaise, that you said was your favourite.
So many happy times we had working together.
Miss you Danny. Sleep tight angel.   Love Irene x

Whilst travelling in Australia, Me and Leo went travelling for a short while and met up with Dan Blake and Jack.. We went to the Sydney aquarium and many other places and although Blake wasn't very happy to see us, Danny and Jack were. That evening Blake had a massive hissy fit as we was all taking too long to get ready and went to bed, but Danny and Jack still took us out to a local bar and we had a lovely time with them. Although we didn't get to know Danny as well and some, he definitely touched on my heart just for being a lovely, caring, generous and wise boy. He knew right from wrong and he certainly knew how to make you laugh! This particular day we went to the aquarium we were talking about reincarnation and what animal we would want to come back as, Danny said he would come back as a Dugong and I took a picture of the boys with their chosen animals. This same day we walked along, I was walking behind with Leo and I said to him Danny is such a lovely boy, he's the type of boy I would want for my daughter to bring home. Never in a million years did we expect him to pass so young, he is very much missed. All I can say now, is even though he's gone these memories still live on and even though we wasn't the best of friends and I didn't know him as well as others, I was so devastated to hear he had passed, it always happens to the BEST ONES .   Love Abbey Xx

---

In August 2012 Danny came to Malia to surprise me Perk and Terry who were out there for the whole summer. None of us had a clue and I remember one day being on our balcony and receiving a call from Dan saying he was in Malia. He told me to leave my apartment and meet him on the Malia strip, but knowing Dan I thought he could be pulling a fast one making me go all that way for him to just be at home in his cabin laughing down the phone at me! So I was sceptical and resorted to asking him the first questions I could think of to prove he was really there. So my first question was along the lines of 'what's the weather like?' Cue laughter from Dan and then he replied 'it's sunny'. Well it's an August day in Greece, so it wasn't exactly going to be anything else was it, as Dan pointed out. I then said something even more stupid like 'are there cloud in the sky?' to which Dan burst out laughing again and said 'NO'. One again, it's an August day in Greece it was always going to be blue skies. At this point I realised I was getting nowhere with my ridiculous questions so decided to storm down to the strip fully prepared for Danny to not be there and to get another call saying how gullible I was!

How wrong I was. I turned up to the strip and there he was, like a covert mission he'd come all the way to Malia without letting us know. I was genuinely so happy! I'd spent two and a half months in Malia with Perk and Terry, and we were starting to tire of it and were heading home in a few days. Dan's arrival brought a new lease of life to the last few days of the trip and we had some of the funniest nights out making our summer trip come to a brilliant end. Without Dan turning up, I think the end of our trip would have just fizzled out.

I remember at the start of one of the nights we decided to go to a quieter bar to watch the opening ceremony of the Olympics. I always remember the Daniel Craig and the Queen sketch and me and Dan nearly falling off our stools in shock and then laughter that the Queen was actually in it! Our final night I don't remember much of as it was a big one, but photos later showed Dan helping to hold me up and take me home. We'd always laugh about those photos and what a state I got myself in!

I'm not ashamed to say that Dan turning up in Malia made me realise just how much I had missed him. Years later we would talk about how he kept it a secret and had told a few of the other boys not to tell us. This was typical Dan, always putting in the effort to make something even more memorable, as his Mum found out when he secretly returned home from Australia after his year travelling! Best times, Jack x

---

I find it hard to put my feelings down on paper, so here goes! I have been part of Dan's life for over 16 years and to pick one memory out of hundreds is quite a difficult thing. My first memory of Dan, was when I wasn't actually part of he's life at the time; I was just a friend of his mum. Danny was about ten years old and was playing a football match one Sunday morning and Shelly asked me to come and watch him, which I did. The final whistle went and Dan came running over to me and his mum. Straight off, he greeted me with "Hi" and then asked his mum who I was. I introduced myself as Rich, a friend of your mum's and added that I was a West Ham scout!! The look on Dan's face was absolutely priceless as his eyes lit up and a massive smile beamed across his face, but I couldn't keep up the pretence for too long and had to come clean and tell him that I was only joking!! The smile quickly disappeared, but

in typical Dan style, he just laughed it off..... Over the years, we would often talk about that moment and laugh.
Love you forever Dan - Rich x

I had the pleasure of meeting Dan through a friend, when I was at university in York. Dan would come up with the other lads for weekends from time to time and it was always such a laugh. From the first time I met him it was clear that Dan was always the centre of the room. He had that kind of magnetic personality that made you just want to be around him.

As I would only see him 2-3 times a year, he always had a back-log of hilarious stories - my favourite will always be the one about the wall getting destroyed on the lad's weekend away in Liverpool and Dan putting his college skills into practice and redecorating!! He told a few of us this story over a few drinks at New Year 2016 and I have honestly never laughed so much in my life!

That night at New Year we spent most of the time doing karaoke - we had a quality night working through the cheesy classics like Westlife & Backstreet Boys. One thing I will never forget is that as Dan was leaving, I started singing I'm forever blowing bubbles to him down the mic and he turned round, came back and finished it off with me. (I'm not even a Hammer fan and Dan always used to take the piss out of the fact I support Grimsby). That was the last time I saw Dan but it is such a great memory and always stays with me. If West Ham are on TV and I hear that song, I always think of Dan and smile to myself.

I had another New Year with Dan (I think two years before) where a group of us ended up in a ropey area of South London at some club. At about 11PM a Michael Jackson impersonator came on - for the first 5 minutes we couldn't stop laughing; it was such a ridiculous situation. But later on everyone just went for it (led by Dan of course). He would always be the one to get everyone else going.

Whenever the boys invited us northern lot down to Essex, one of our first questions would be 'is Dan and that coming out?' He always seemed like the leader of the gang to me and it was quality when he was there. If Dan was involved you knew the other lads would be too and we all have loads of ace memories of the whole group of lads.

A classic was the time Dan met us for a quiet pint after work – a few of us had been on a day session and Dan said he would meet us for one. One led to two and then a few more and the next thing, we are in Reflex in central London - Dan is in full work gear and has had to convince the bouncer to let him stash his tool bag in the cloak room - I'd never seen that before and I'm laughing now as I type this!!! We stayed in there until it closed and got the night bus home together, tool bag and all!! Alfie.

Danny was never one to shy away from a night out, whether that was a local night out or a couple of drinks after work in the city. Saying that, a couple of drinks usually meant a late one in Reflex, sometimes with work the next day. On numerous occasions after a night out we'd end up in Dan's cabin, slightly worse for wear, watching children's films. This was after Jim had already walked past his own home after a 2 mile walk from Romford and Dan always shouting out goodnight to Jim's mum at 3 in the morning. On this walk we'd all attempt our best techno Viking impressions. Dan sat in front of the TV for a good 30 minutes trying to re-enact a scene from the film, Rango and we couldn't go to sleep until he'd mastered it. Terry took over and captured it in one go. Michelle would come down the following morning to the smell of alcohol and kebabs. We'd then make our way for a breakfast and a pint of coke to cure the hangovers! Love James x

---

When we were going to USA, Dan and I got on the plane and we were right at the front, sitting on the bulk head seats. We sat down and were getting ready for our flight whilst other people were still boarding. Just as we thought everyone had finished boarding, a lady suddenly came running down the tunnel towards the plane with her suitcase in tow, clearly fearing she was going to miss her flight. As she literally jumped into the plane, she lost her footing and with suitcase flying, she face palmed the floor!! What followed was two loud screams! The first was from the lady herself as she lay in the aisle, being speedily assisted by the air hostesses, who were clambering around her to see if she was alright. The second scream was Dan and I! This scream was quickly followed with full on laughter at what had just happened in front of us and then a feeling of slight guilt that we had been unable to control ourselves at this lady's misfortune.

Fortunately, the lady was fine and no damage was done. She got up and headed off to her seat whilst Dan and I kept playing this face palming moment in our heads for the duration of the flight! Steven x

When my Megan said she had met a young man called Danny Brown from Essex on a night out in Liverpool, I didn't really think much about it. I was a bit surprised when she said they were keeping in touch on Facebook. Then when she said she was going to Essex to meet up with Danny again....I was worried sick and demanded she get his full address and telephone number for me. Meg was mortified and refused until I threatened to contact Danny or his mum myself. So, Danny gave Meg his address to give to me. Trust was formed and I felt better. When Meg returned from Essex she was beaming and already in love. Seeing your child so happy is the best feeling ever. Not long after, Meg invited Danny to our home in Liverpool to meet us.

He popped his head around the door and said hello. I remember his huge smile and twinkling eyes. I gave him a hug and thought awwww, Megs done good! He was so polite, chatty and relaxed around us. Seeing Meg and Danny together, snuggled on the sofa and holding hands was so cute. I knew their relationship was going to be special. So glad Meg met Danny and found out how beautiful being in love can be. Love always, Joanne Xxx

From Dan's 18th birthday onwards, a crowd of us including myself, Dan, Jim, Jade, Grant and Charlie would regularly go to Romford on a Thursday night. Usually starting off in Yates or Missoula and then heading on to either Liquid, Envy or Kosho. Our many evenings out included seeing The Wanted, Roll Deep, Miss Dynamite and Example, though Jim and I had left before Example had even came on stage! Once, Dan was so drunk before we had even left Yates, he fell down the steep wooden spiral staircase, but he would tell you it wasn't him. We went to many foam parties and ended up walking home freezing cold and soaking wet, as no cabs or buses would take us. On our nights out, whether we walked home as the sun rose or got a bus or cab, Dan, ever the gentlemen - even while drunk, always made sure I got to my door okay, often going out of his way to do so.

For Shelly's Halloween party in 2015, Dan and I deliberated his costume for weeks, he finally settled on the evil witch from Snow White, and charged me with creating his outfit - sourcing the cape, basket, even the hair extensions! He was so disappointed that he would probably have to shave off his beard for the make-up, but he took it seriously and did so. He came to time to get ready and sat quietly as I created my masterpiece. That night, I did 5 faces; including my own, and even with terry and Dan both turning up late- as usual - we got it done in time. Everyone made an incredible effort with costumes that night, although it's a shame he didn't manage to spray paint Luna white, like he said he would! Miss you, my bum chum, Dolly x

---

Hi, my name is Shelley and I am Danny's cousin from Australia.

It's taken me far too long to send this email and I apologise. I have been meaning to email you for some time now but knew I would find it hard to try and put my memories on paper without having a good cry as I think of Dan (although I think of him every day).

I knew of Dan but hadn't met him until a day while he was in Australia, I asked him to catch a train down to my home town of Wollongong so we could spend the weekend together. It just so happened that I had tickets to a concert that same weekend, which meant we booked a couple of nights down in Canberra, where we would do the touristy thing and I would show him Australia's capital city, then we would also catch the concert.

Dan caught the train down from Sydney and basically 5 minutes after meeting we were in the car on the way to Canberra – a 3 hour car trip! During that 3 hour trip, we laughed like we had known each other our entire lives and talked non-stop about our love for family and life (although most of the trip was also Dan telling me my taste in music was "shithouse")

I didn't have the heart to tell him at the time, but half the conversation I didn't understand because I couldn't understand his accent but we made it work!! We finally reached Canberra and checked into our hotel. The next day we toured around Canberra, parliament house, the War Memorial and everywhere else touristy there is to go in Canberra. Just by the lake in Canberra there is an International Flag display where every flag from around the world is displayed. I stupidly bet Dan he couldn't name them all and bet him a lunch on it – I lost. To my amazement he named every single flag and country so I had to shout him a beer and a 'Snitty' at the pub!

That night I took him to a concert for a band named Bernard Fanning – needless to say he hated it but we still laughed! After the show had finished we were drinking in a nearby pub and the band walked in, I was absolutely star struck and flatly refused to go up to them, not Dan. Off he went and before I knew it we were at their table for hours drinking and laughing and partying the night away – that was just Dan's way – he got on with anybody and everybody.

The next morning we both woke up and neither of us could remember the night before events – both of us were in single beds surrounded by McDonald's wrappers (my bank account later revealed we spent something like $50.00 on McDonalds that night, which for 2 people is insane). We had to check our phones for photos and messages to see where the night had led. One of the photos I had was Dan standing next to a water fountain. I don't know what we found so funny here but I do recall laughing all night till my sides hurt.

We drove home the next day (a much quieter trip than the one down, due to us both feeling extremely unwell) and Dan hopped back on a train to Sydney. This memory (the first one I have of Dan) is still one of my all-time favourites and Dan and I used to laugh about that night out often.

 Dan and I caught up as many times as we could while he was in Australia and I truly loved him. Every time we caught up – Bastille concert / an AFL game / in Darwin, it always resulted in a great laugh and a couple of beers. When I dropped him off at the airport to fly home I cried the 2 hour car trip home – I knew I was going to miss him greatly.

When he returned to the UK, Dan and I still spoke but only rarely which I now look back on and regret.......... but I know he knew I loved him, I think of him daily and talk to him often. To his family reading this he loved you all so dearly and spoke so much of you – his Mum /

Dad / Step Dad and siblings, and through stories he told me I felt like I somehow know all of you. Love to you all, Shelley x

---

Danny's knowledge of Netflix' series was known to all and we all looked to him to choose our next show. His favourites included Breaking Bad, Prison Break, Walking Dead, Lost, Entourage, Game of Thrones and Suits to name a few. A couple of months ago I went into Danny's room only to find out all his Netflix viewing was at my expense, as I noticed my own name in the top corner – he had been poncing off my account and had shared the login details with the rest of the boys! Ryan x

---

The first time I met Danny was at football many years ago, I was playing for Leaside and one game Danny arrived. My dad and I honestly remember that day, because of Danny! Coming on from the bench and scoring a goal of the season contender with one of his first touches on his debut! (After the game I said to my dad "wow, who is the new boy?) As it was so long ago, I wasn't sure if people remembered it and hadn't really spoken to Danny about it since. It made me smile when I heard at the funeral that it was remembered, and that Danny didn't let people forget it! From his first game, Danny went on to be one of the best goal scorers I've ever played football with. Matt.

I have a lifetime of memories with Danny, and I'm struggling to figure out the "best one" which perfectly expresses him. However I believe this would be impossible as one memory would never summarise the diverse and distinctive person that Danny was.

A memory that makes me smile every time was, ironically, when my cat Tiggy died, I must have been 8 or 9, making Danny 10 or 11. I was playing The Sims at the time in Danny's room when Rich & Danny came up and sat next to me on the floor, leaning on the side of the chair. Danny and I could not be trusted sharing the computer independently so we had a time limit, an hour each alternately I assume I can't vividly remember, but my time was nearly up. Rich looked at me and said my name, I turned to look at him and Dan sitting next to me, faces sorrowful, "Amber's died, you know she wasn't very well but the vets called Mummy today and told her the news." said Rich. I started to get upset, obviously, Rich just sat there giving the typical "helpful" shoulder rub you give when there's bad news. Danny however knew exactly what would help my grieving heart by assuring me "It's alright Becky, you don't have to come off 'Sims' now, I will let you play it a bit longer!!"

It makes me laugh now as it sounds such a silly thing to try and comfort someone. This sums up Danny more than most things, if there was something he could do to help you, no matter how big or small, he would do it without giving it a second thought. He knew he was sacrificing an hour of Football Manager for his distraught little sister. He couldn't take away my upset, but he knew what might make it better, even if it just took my mind off of it for a while. Love you always Dan, you were my first ever friend and will forever be my brother - Becky, x

---

The last time I saw Danny was back at Charlie's birthday drinks late last year. Although, we've known all the boys for years it can still be a bit awkward at first as we hadn't seen most of them since Charlie's last birthday! Soon after meeting the boys, I luckily ended up next to Danny at the bar. We quickly started talking and soon it was 45 minutes later. Talking to Danny was always easy as he was down to earth, funny and genuine.

I wish I could've been able to remember something poignant from that conversation, but it was just a long overdue catch up, we just spoke about work, girlfriends, holidays etc. However, I can remember reminding my mates at the end of the night that, "Danny is well alright."

We need more people like Danny in the world today. He was a real credit to you! Thinking of your family always! Alfie

---

I worked with Danny at William Hill for a few years when he first started with the company. We had many laughs together at all the strange people that would come into our shop, I'm only 8 years older than Dan remember this for my story,

So I had a day off Dan was working and a customer asked him 'is that GINGER lady that works here your MUM!!! So instead of him saying, no don't be silly she is only 8 years older than me, he decided to play along and said yes!! What a cheek!!

Next day I returned to work in the morning Dan come in at 1 o'clock and said hello mum!! I didn't have a clue what had been said after him telling me and me calling him a cheeky sod, I did laugh a lot!

From that day on he never called me by my name always mum, and not just at work, he would do it if he saw me in the pub or street or wherever our a paths crossed! He even got me a mum birthday card once, so in the end I gave in and started calling him Son!! That memory will stay with me forever. Caroline Xxx

---

Dan, I remember when you drove us to the station and we got the train to Upton Park with Steve to watch the West Ham v Liverpool match, in the FA Cup 4th round. We won that game 2-1 and everyone started chanting at the Liverpool fans, to the tune of 'You'll never walk alone' with the words replaced as 'Sign on, sign on with a pen in your hand and you'll never get a job'!! The whole stadium was singing it and I thought it was absolutely brilliant and was laughing so much with you! I asked you why they were singing it and you said "Because no one in Liverpool has a job, Regan... Well except for Meg!!" It was one of so many memories that I have of you, Steve and me going to the football, but this is one of my favourites.

I will always remember how you used to eat your spaghetti bolognaise quicker than me and then start poking your fork into my dinner and taking little bits of spaghetti off my plate! I would get all panicky thinking you were going to eat it all!! I couldn't kick the football around in the garden without you coming out of your cabin and joining in and showing me some skills and how I would sit in your room with you watching you play your PS4 and if we played two player, you would have to keep stopping to rescue me cause I would keep getting shot if we were playing Call of Duty.

I love and miss you so much every day Dan xx. Forever your brother, Regan x

I would quite often bump into Danny whilst travelling on the district line on my way to and from work! He would always brighten up my day with some funny story about something that had happened to him or his mates at the weekend or he would almost certainly banter with me about the fact that I was part-time and only had to travel into London two days a week and that wasn't really working!! One particular journey home from work will always make me smile when I think of Dan! I had got on the District Line at Mile End and for once had actually got myself a seat! I got out my trashy celebrity magazine and started to read it. If ever I bumped into Dan on the journey home it would usually be when he got on at West Ham. On this particular occasion I had been so engrossed in my magazine that I hadn't noticed Dan get on the tube and silently sit down next to me. He then proceeded to read over my shoulder all the way from West Ham to Barking without me noticing and then when he couldn't hold in his laugh anymore - he tapped me on the shoulder and said "are you ignoring me or what?!". He thought it was so funny and we giggled about it the rest of the journey home!

Not only will I remember Dan for his laugh, his smile, his jokes, his winding me up about my obsession with Olly Murs.... but also for his kindness. I remember chatting with Dan one evening when I was round there about a film I had been watching that had lost the sound about 15 minutes before the end and kept freezing at the same point so I didn't know how it ended and it was really annoying as it had been such a good film! I had spent ages trying to find it on the internet and looking on other channels to see if i could find out the ending but with no luck! A few days later I had a message to say that Dan had found it and had saved it on a memory stick for me to watch! I will never forget that kindness. Love Tracy x

Dan,

After school I then disappeared off the face of the earth according to you because I went into full time work doing my hairdressing then went out to Spain. When I then came back home I'll never forget me coming round with Jim to your dads for a party and you saying "I never thought I'd see you again Em, thought you'd died". I then remember many twitter messages between us about if I'm staying in England for Jim to start a life together, once I said yes you were all excited and was asking if I officially loved him and when will you be hearing wedding bells lol! Then of course you left us to go to Oz, I remember talking to you about it when you was debating whether to go and I said you only live once Dan you've got to do it, you can always come back home if it's not for you. We lost our leader as soon as you left on the plane and were totally lost without you. Every gathering we tried to sort out was an epic fail and we used to laugh saying "When's Dan back to sort out our plans"? As soon as you mentioned you were on your way home, I remember saying to Jim that's it, we'll get in the car and go pick him up from the airport as it was all a secret, but Ryan beat us to it!!

Jim was so annoyed! Love you, Emily x

Michael, Jim and I first met Danny when he was 4 years old at Primary school. For those of us who went to Primary School, Danny was a central part of our childhood. Danny was mischievous, funny and always easy to get on with, apart from the one time when he punched me on the nose over the park, for what I can't remember now! But I can safely say he did have a good right-hander.

What we will always remember is that meeting Danny at such a young age ensured the enjoyment of countless laughs and thrills, many that our parents probably wouldn't have been best pleased with, which obviously made them all the more enjoyable.

Memories for me include the long summers spent in Danny's garden, often jumping and doing flips off of his shed into a swimming pool. Or 'playing out' on the nearby streets, which translates into annoying neighbours by playing knock down ginger (Danny always was the fastest runner) or unscrewing and collecting the dust caps off of the newest cars that we would spot on our travels.

These shared experiences created a deep bond through which we all knew Danny always had our back. A particular time when he helped me was when we went away on a weekend trip with the Scouts. Still young at the age of 9 I quickly became very homesick and upset I wasn't sharing a room with Danny. Danny, with his unique ability to immediately get on and have fun with people he'd only just met, not so much. However he took time and care in talking to me and cheering me up to ensure a great trip. That was Danny in a nutshell to me. Miss you my friend. Phil x

~~~~~~~~~~~~~~~~~

One day in the six weeks holiday aged 9, along with Dan, Simon and Phil, I found myself in Harrow Lodge Park looking for something to do. Simon came up with the idea of a - and I quote - "stone war". This consisted of two teams – Dan and me, against Phil and Simon. Our war zone was the tennis courts and the objective was to throw small rocks at each other to potentially injure each other. Simon was running low on ammo and proceeded to the no go zone to collect more stones. As Simon was reloading, Dan, who had a brilliant throw on him, threw a perfect dart like shot which popped Simon right on the temple. Blood poured from a gaping wound and an almighty scream came from our downed enemy. We quickly realised how serious this was and rushed Simon to Dan's house, where his mum collected him and took him home to recover. To this day I'm proud to say me and Dan remain undefeated in our stone war battles!! Love Jim x

---

One of my favourite stories I tell about Danny, and I used to tell him this many times, is that I wasn't actually sure about him when I first knew of him at school!

I joined in year 7 from Sutton's and didn't really know anyone other than from my primary school. For most of my first year, I kind of just stuck to people from my primary school and people in my form so didn't really mix with anyone else.

I'd seen Danny around school but didn't know much about him. It was in the summer between years 7-8 that one friend said something about Danny hanging around with a kid called Joe, as they were friends from school. Although I kept myself to myself, everyone knew Joe as a bit of a wrong'un, so I used to avoid him at all costs! Hearing Danny's name being mentioned as Joe's mate made me wary of him and so I thought he was someone else I'd avoid!

I didn't know any of the Bernhurst boys in general other than Phil, who was in my form. Phil asked me and Charlie that summer, to come out with him and his mates and meet them at "the den" over Harrow Lodge.

I walked into the Den and I remember Danny was climbing up a tree. I walked in a bit sheepish and no word of a lie I still remember Dan's first ever words to me as, "Oi, give me that pen". I looked on the floor and there was a marker pen so I passed it to Danny, who then scribbled something like his name onto the tree. Not a good start I thought, definitely a wrong'un like Joe, and I don't remember speaking to him much more that day...

Few weeks later, we started year 8 and they mixed the classes. I got put into a science group with Danny and somehow ended up sitting next to him. We had Dr Mardi, which basically meant we learnt nothing and every class turned out to be me and Dan just having a right old laugh chatting absolute nonsense! Just silly things like one time we realised one of the science books was written by a bloke called Dirk (can't remember last name) and at the time me and Dan both followed basketball and there was a player called Dirk Nowtiski...so for some reason we used to refer to each other as Dirk in this drawn out stupidly deep voice. I'd turn up to a lesson and it would be "Alright Diiiirk" or Dan would be like "You coming out later Diiiirk". I remember one day Dr Mardi sending me to a tiny table where the computer was in the corner of the room, because I was chatting so much. About 5 minutes later Danny got sent to the same table, so we could carry on chatting nonsense! We then put our pens under the keyboard keys and flicked them up hitting the ceiling just to spite Dr Mardi, which we obviously thought was hilarious!

Me and Dan become really good mates so quickly and started to walk home together within a few weeks of starting year 8 and I was then going out with Dan and everyone else most week nights. I loved that Dan lived near me too, as it meant we'd walk home together after a night out and have some great chats on the way! Usually, we would be moaning about how bad the night had been, but we'd still end up over the park the next day!

To this day, I don't think I've ever been proven wrong about a person more than I was about Danny, just shows you can't judge someone because of who they hang around with, plus it turned out that he didn't even hang around with Joe much anymore!!) It's funny to think that although I was cautious about Danny, I can't ever remember becoming mates with someone so quick! That says all you need to know about Danny - so friendly, comfortable to be around and fucking Hilarious! I'll never forget how welcoming he was to me when I used to go out with him and the boys..

I always used to remind Dan about how I thought he was a bit of a wrong'un when I first met him, and he'd just proper laugh about it and I'm so glad I was proved wrong! Love Jack.

I remember how we used to meet up at the local Harvester and then head into Romford for a night out with a group of mates. This night was no different, we followed the same steps we always did and ended up in Missoula bar, in Romford. Our mixed group of boys and girls were chatting as we normally would, when suddenly; one of the girls in the group shouted "Oh No". Perplexed we asked what was wrong, to which *she replied that there was a guy in the club, who had very drunkenly tried it on with her the week before and that she didn't want to see him again! We all laughed as she told us the story about the failed attempt of this drunken guy wanting to buy her a drink and as well as curious, we asked her to point out, who this guy was. My heart literally sank, when she pointed directly at Dan. "That's my brother" I shouted, everyone, including me started to laugh, except for this girl, who must have felt like she' just dug the biggest hole possible!*

It wasn't till the next morning that I told Dan the story of the night before, Dan being Dan denied the lot, except the being drunk part! Love you always, Steve x

---

Danny,

I can remember sitting at the dining table with you and we were having Essex Grill for dinner and you dared me to eat one of the green chillies for a fiver. I was a little hesitant at first but then grabbed the smallest chilli on the plate! And instead of taking a small piece I stupidly decided to eat the entire thing!! My tongue started to burn and my face went bright red. I can remember you laughing at my red scrunched up face.

It took you weeks to give me that fiver, but after nagging you about it constantly, I eventually wore you down and you gave it to me!! I will love you forever Dan, miss you so much, your little sister, Meggie xx

---

There's too many memories but a couple of my favourites are our last game of Leaside, when I was too hung-over to play but Dan was so keen to win he played in defence and I went upfront - he wouldn't let me live that one down (and also blamed Phil as he's the reason I was out drinking Gin the night before).

Another is when we were in Malia and Dan hooked up with a Swedish girl on the beach! The next morning he woke up with what he called 'spots on his manhood' and wasn't sure what to do, so he told me in confidence! I just couldn't stop laughing and said that the Swede must have given him a present! Thankfully and once checked, it later turned out to be just a heat rash.

The other good memories consist of Dan discovering his love for 'mud slides' (a mix of vodka and baileys) which in our teens he wouldn't let us go a night out without having one! And who could forget when we tried to get that cream leather reclining arm chair into his cabin... Trying to get in through the hallway and it was obvious it wasn't going to fit when it got stuck on the banisters and against the wall, we tried and tried and in the end resulted in taking it back out the front door and asking a neighbour if we could lift it over the fence! Hilarious, Charlie x

---

Even throughout his time at Primary School, Dan had that cheeky smile that would radiate the room, this never changed as he grew up. At his time in Benhurst, Dan was involved in various clubs but in particular football and his love of it whether this was playing or as he grew up, going to watch his beloved West Ham. A memory that sticks in my head from our time in primary was going to Dan's house and without our parents knowing, we watched the South Park movie, which contained some rather bad language and swear words which we thought were hilarious! This led to us quoting lines and songs from that film for the next 20 years. Benhurst Primary was the start of an incredible journey for me and Dan. Our friendship continued to grow and to be mates for such a long time with such a caring, kind and funny person meant the absolute world to me growing up with him by my side. Miss you everyday mate, Mike x

---

I have a billion memories of Danny, accumulated over his lifetime with me. So many memories were typical 'had to be there' moments but just a couple that recently sprung to mind were these....

The first goes back to when Danny was about 7 or 8 years old. Becky, who was nearly 5 at that time, had been sent a bag of clothes from a friend of mine, whose daughter had outgrown the items,. In this bag was quite a lot of clothing but the one thing that stood out was a beautiful red velvet dress with lace cuffs. Becky was trying everything on and saying what she did and didn't like, when all of a sudden Danny came flying into the lounge wearing this red velvet dress!! It had a full skirt on it and he proceeded to spin around in circles in the lounge marvelling at the range of the fullness and height that the dress reached!! Oh my, we laughed about that moment on so many occasions with him as he got older!!

The other memory was literally weeks before he passed away when we were out up London and on our way back, Dan said he was hungry. We were passing a Beigel bar and I suggested getting something from there. We walked up and the lady asked me what I'd like, I looked at the large chalked menu on the wall, not seeing what I wanted, I said "Can I have a bacon roll"? The woman looked at me a bit strangely as I heard Dan say "Mum"!!, I looked at him and he had a classic look of bemusement and a bit of shock thrown in for good measure, across his face as he said "Beigel's, they're Jewish... They don't do bacon"!! Suddenly the penny dropped and as Dan started to grin and stifle a laugh as the woman said "I can do you halal sausage"? I nodded my head and said "Lovely, thank you" as Danny quickly added "Make that two please". I can still hear him laughing as he shook his head in disbelief as we walked with our Halal sausage Beigel's to the station.

Such priceless, and beautiful memories that will never leave us, love you forever sweetheart, Mum x

---

For Danny's birthday weekend in 2016, we set out on the seemingly perfect weekend up to Liverpool. Danny travelled up to Liverpool alone ahead of us boys so that he could meet his girlfriend Megan. We arrived Friday evening and met Danny at an apartment, before heading out to the karaoke bar "Woody's" and inevitably ending up at the favourite "Popworld". Popworld is a great place to go if you don't take yourself too seriously and enjoy the old classics - Dan loved it.

We arrived back at the apartment early hours of Saturday morning, looking forward to going to Goodison Park just a few hours later for Everton v West Ham. James and I were in the lounge area, after I had successfully carried him back to the apartment, when a small drunken scuffle ended up with James crashing into the plasterboard wall and forming a human outline in it! My mind flashed straight to the £500 deposit that was being held from Dan's account, and with that, I promptly went and brought him into review and assess the situation. I remember his face when he looked at it - a combination of minor disappointment but with a strong underlying chuckle. We all decided the best option was to go to sleep and worry about it in the morning!

Sunrise came and I was awoken by "Who's smashed the wall up!" I walked from my bed to the lounge, passing some urine on the carpet and a pair of boxer shorts covered in vomit, which were hanging upon the mantel piece like a proud trophy! Danny had forgotten all about the night before and suddenly reality had set in! So for a while, we considered our options:

1. Be honest and tell the apartment owners
2. Fix the wall
3. Disguise the evidence

Dan's favourite option was number 3 - within minutes he arrived in the lounge carrying a 6 foot long mirror and explained how this would completely disguise the damage and nobody would ever notice it! Although there was some logic here, I found this hilarious that we thought nobody would realise that the mirror which once sat proudly at the apartment entrance to greet the guests had been moved and was now hanging in the lounge! We eventually settled on a combination of 2 and 3!

Myself, Danny, Steve and Terry were off to the football, and we left James to procure some filler, sanding blocks and paint, his initial feedback was that this was hard to come by in Liverpool city centre!

We got to Goodison really hung-over from alcohol, as well as the tricky situation we had got ourselves into! It was a very poor game and West Ham were losing 2-0 by the 56th minute against 10 men. I looked across to Dan and he was sat with his hoodie over his head. We've always been ones to join in with the chants and get behind the teams, but this was a different day. Soon came the 78th minute, still 2-0 but West Ham launched an attack and made it 2-1. Suddenly the game turned on its head - the West Ham fans realised we had 10 minutes to get another goal against 10 men. Dan stood up and his hoodie was down. We immediately scored a second goal and it was 2-2! We were all going mad in the away end - singing our hearts out and pushing the team on to get a winner. It was the 90th minute and Sakho played it back to Payet who nipped in a winner! 3-2! What followed was the maddest and one of the happiest moments I've experienced. The West Ham players came over to their fans at the final whistle and celebrated the turnaround with us. We were all stood on our chairs singing "We've got Payet" on loop for approximately 45 minutes!

The headache of the apartment was forgotten for a good hour or two. We left the stadium and caught up with James, who had little success and soon we all found ourselves in Pound world. We settled on buying a timber furniture paint, which was no colour match for the wall whatsoever, but it was this or nothing. Arriving back at the room, we all put our faith in Dan to deliver a masterpiece. "Dan it's time to show us all those skills you developed in during your three years of painting and decorating at college". We were under equipped with tools - Dan was applying filler with his finger and sanding it down with the cheapest sand paper in existence. We joked that the toilet roll might have been a better option! Sand, fill, paint, repeat was the vibes for the next couple of hours. We went out again for the night and put the worry to the back of our heads yet again. We had convinced ourselves that Dan had done a fairly good job with the tools and materials that he had.

The next morning at sunrise, we opened the curtains. "OMG" was the general comment. The sunlight caused the human body figure to stand out as if it was a monument! The shape of the indent, plus the failed colour match was devastating. Dan's response was "Somebody get me a roller and I'll paint the whole apartment to tie the colour in". We were all in hysterics, but this seemed viable! We went back to the previous day's tactic of sand, fill, paint, repeat, before checking our watches -

"Shit! We have to check out in an hour!" The paint was still wet; there was plaster dust from sanding the wall all over the floor and on the bed sheets that we had put down for dust sheets! We swiftly agreed to ring up for an extension to our check out and after a bit of haggling, we managed to agree a few vital hours.

There was nothing more we could physically do and we realised our only chance of possibly getting away with this was now to visit option 3 - Get rid of the evidence. We bagged up all tools and materials, cleared every spec of loose paint and dust. We then explored the tactics behind getting caught and realised if we made the rest of the apartment look spectacularly clean and tidy, there would be no reason for anybody to walk past this point. We'd gone from "Cowboy builders" to "60 minute makeover" within seconds as we set upon making the place presentable. We convinced ourselves that if there was no evidence, only a damaged (but made good) wall, then surely the owners wouldn't expect five guys on a weekend away to be carrying out decorating works?!

Upon leaving the apartment, we took the bag of evidence and put it in a bin in a nearby building site. Had we pulled off the spectacular? There was a definite sense of accomplishment amongst us, but we couldn't settle on whether it was the equivalent of the Italian Job robbery or Mr Bean damaging the Mona Lisa painting!

We returned to London and held tight for a few days but the deposit wasn't refunded. Then a smug WhatsApp message came through from Danny and I knew it had been returned! However, Dan was slightly pissed off that they had added a £20 parking charge, even though we'd gone up by train! Happily, we let them have this, on the knowledge that we had received the full deposit back.

That was a truly great weekend and probably my most memorable with Danny. Love you mate, Grant x

---

I am the luckiest girl in the world to have found Dan, my soul mate. He is the first person I have ever been in love with and will be my only true love, always. I will miss him for the rest of my life and everything I do will be for Danny, my inspiration. When I first met Dan outside Popworld, the first thing that attracted me to him was his beautiful, cheeky smile and charming personality. He held my hand in and out of the taxi like the gentleman he is and we bonded over our love for Game of thrones. I added him on Facebook a few hours after meeting him and we spoke all day every day for the next 2 years we had together. Dan was funny, kind, happy, genuine, thoughtful, caring and charming. He was just an all around beautiful person. It didn't take much persuasion from him for me to come down to Essex to see him. We had the best weekend when I first came to Essex to visit and I definitely fell in love with him that weekend so easily. Dan was such a warm and loving person, I felt like I was home when I was with him. Every time we spent together was quality time and we made it so special.

Dan and I shared a love of travelling. We made the most of our time together by going on the most amazing adventures. We first went to Dubrovnik, the main attraction being the tour of king's landing, a fictional place from game of thrones which I and Dan absolutely loved. We walked along the walls of Dubrovnik to the end only to realize we missed a vital part from the show. We walked back down the narrow path of the wall with annoyed passersby telling us we were going the wrong way for Dan go shout and reply "yes thanks, we know", as we barged past!

Our second trip was to Marrakech. Our second favourite holiday! The highlight of this being the 9 hour journey we made to the edge of the Sahara, finally climbing onto camels to ride further into the desert. I gave Dan my phone as he had a backpack to put it in but he decided to use it to take pictures (which I'm glad he did). I couldn't look back at Dan on his camel in fear that I was going to lose my balance and fall off but I could still see Danny's shadow to the side of me and there he was with one hand on the camel and one holding my phone taking selfies! I was telling him to please use both hands, as I was worried he was going to either drop my phone or worse fall off the bloody camel! But Dan being Dan laughed it off. Once again, I looked to the side and could see Dan's shadow but this time he had both hands off the camel, laughing and saying "No hands!" He did make me laugh but my heart was in my mouth. We arrived at the camp and it was the most amazing experience as we watched the sun set over the hills of the Sahara desert and it was spent with the best person.

The following morning we made our way back to the hotel. One stop we made we were introduced to another camel. We decided to get a picture taken just in front of the camel. Dan positioned us both to what he thought was a 'safe' distance from the camel and there we stood smiling for the camera. Next minute my head was pulled back with my hair in the camel's teeth! I pulled my head forward away from the camel to see Dan totally shocked, but I could tell he was struggling not to laugh!

Danny was so impulsive and loved surprising me as much as I loved to surprise him. He would just turn up in Liverpool, completely unannounced whilst I was working, or surprising me with a trip away somewhere. I remember coming home from work one night, I walked into my house and was greeted by the dog at the door, as I looked up Dan was standing in the kitchen door way with that beaming smile! I gave him the biggest hug, I was always so excited and happy to see him, he made me the happiest I will ever be. In October 2016 he took me to New York for my 20th birthday and we had the time of our lives. He made sure we got to see and do everything we wanted. We were both absolutely knackered coming home, but it was worth it and I will treasure the memories he gave me forever.

Danny and I spent two Christmases together. One was in Essex and one in Liverpool and both of them were just perfect. I couldn't have asked for anything better. Our last Christmas together in Liverpool was when I bought Dan a tablet with built in projector. He was so happy with it, but it was always hard buying him presents and then trying to keep it a surprise, because he'd always be so close to buying it for himself! I used *to say that I could never surprise him, but it went well that year! Because I didn't have a projector or a screen, unlike inspector gadget Dan, we always used to have to watch films through the tablet, with the projector facing the bedroom ceiling, creating our very own cinema!! It was here where we first watched Moana, his guilty pleasure and favourite Disney film. I'd always catch him singing, humming and whistling the songs and even found it on his recently played list on Spotify!*

For my Christmas present, Danny had booked us tickets to go to Krakow in Poland. This was somewhere we had always wanted to go and I'm so glad we both got the chance to go together.

Being season ticket holders, Dan and I attended nearly all the games together and one particular match sticks with me. We went to watch the West Ham v Watford, just after we had moved to the new stadium. West Ham were playing amazing and during this game, the ball went through Mark Noble and out wide to Dimitry Payet. What Payet did next was pure magic. He flicked the ball past a player and performed the Rabona trick (Google it), before crossing it into Michail Antonio to header the ball into the back of the net. The crowd erupted at the goal! Immediately, I started to sing "We've got Payet, Dimitry Payet, I just don't think you understand. He's super Slav's man, he's better than Zidane, we've got Dimitry Payet". Dan joined in, accompanied by Grant and several people sitting near us. Gradually it got louder and was travelling further around the stadium, ending up with the whole stadium singing the song.

Feeling pretty proud of myself, I looked at Dan who had a huge smile on his face as he turned to me and simply said "That was alright wasn't it"! That was it, we turned to face the pitch and carried on watching the rest of the game, but the look on Dan's face followed by what he said to me, I can relive that moment like it was yesterday. Steve x

Dan,

We never got to say goodbye and I didn't feel it was my right to speak on your 'Day', but I will forever treasure that last evening meal of just the two of us sat together, eating and talking. I clearly recall us being joined by Regan and me watching and listening to the pair of you laughing at the YouTube videos he was showing you. You helped me print off the Italy tickets and then with a "See you later", you wandered off down your room to watch the football.

Had I have spoken on 'Danny's Day'; this is all I would have said....

My darling Dan, I feel very privileged to have been part of your life for so many years and very proud to call you my son. I never wanted to be called Dad or Step Dad, just Rich was enough. You always made it so easy to love you, from that caring and funny little boy, who grew into the most amazing adult. I feel we had a special bond and I hope you felt that too. I loved that you would always ask me for my opinion and ask me for advice. You will always be my best friend and I am completely heartbroken that you have been taken from us. I love you and miss you so much Dan and I still can't quite believe you have actually gone and that I will never see or speak to you again xx

Love you always, forever my son, Rich x

Darling Danny

It's so hard to write a letter to you my darling, knowing that you will never read it. Since you have been gone, I have sent so many texts to your phone and messaged you my fears, thoughts and feelings to your memorialised Facebook account, all of which will forever remain unopened. Sometimes when I speak to you the only words I can find is to tell you how much I miss you. I hope you hear my words, because I know you would be asking me not to cry as much as I do, but my heart is broken darling and that can never be repaired now you are gone.

In my head I have tried countless times to place you somewhere in the world, either out with your friends, back in Australia, visiting Meg in Liverpool or telling myself you are at work, just to make a bad day bearable. But you aren't in the world anymore and reality of knowing that is excruciatingly painful. You occupy my thoughts for about 85% of the day. You are the first thought when I wake in the morning and you are the last as I close my eyes at night. Everywhere I go you are with me. I visualise you walking out of the station when I drive past it, remembering all the times you sent cheeky texts on your late night train journeys home, asking me if I'd come and pick you up. I sit at traffic lights in town and can remember the countless occasions I dropped you off when you were meeting up with friends. I look out of the kitchen window and can see you walking up the garden with your work bag on your shoulder and your overflowing laundry basket hooked on your arm, always desperately trying to open the gate, while wrestling with Luna to get in the house without getting covered in dog fur. I hear a key in the front door and still after all these months, my heart is willing for it to be you who will walk in. I hear the siren of an ambulance racing somewhere and it takes me right back to those first ten minutes after finding you, when they were rushing to you. There are a million things I miss about you every day darling. I miss wondering what time you'll be home from work, I miss hearing you ask me to leave your dinner in the oven, because you are in the middle of an online game. I miss our conversations about everything and nothing. I miss your wisdom and your wit, your giggle, your sarcasm and your unmistakable laugh. I miss hearing about your day and what pissed you off or what made you laugh, I miss your moaning about how I always paired your clean socks up into the wrong pairs. I miss cooking your favourite dinners and your weekly whinge about always having sausage and chips on a Monday night or how you liked a fried egg but without the yolk! I miss your smell and I miss hearing you slam the patio door whenever you entered the house or went down to your room. I miss watching you running down the garden to your cabin in the rain, hilariously trying to avoid the snails on the grass, whilst punching the air in celebration and calling out how many you had accidently trodden on en route! I just really miss you darling, every single day.

We have all become so different since you went away Dan. I hardly recognise the person I was. I remember her, but am brutally aware of the fact that she is no longer here. There are moments when a little bit of the old me seems to resurface, but those moments come and go and last as long as water being poured onto a sandy beach. I don't really look forward to anything anymore, I'm no longer spontaneous and I don't laugh a fraction of the amount that I used to. I don't make plans and I don't go out and see the friends I had, not like I used to. I loved being the Mum I was to you, Steven, Becky, Megan and Regan and although I am forever a mum of five, now I'm only a mum to four. We all see life differently now, we don't worry about meaningless things or situations. We are learning to change what we can, and accept what we can't. We have all adopted the 'live for the moment' attitude. The 'Danny affect' has influenced many of your friends to grab the opportunity to travel, as well as Steven, who is making plans to go to Canada for a year with Nic. Your Meg applied and has been accepted to go to university for three years and study zoology, which is absolutely fantastic for her, because you know more than anyone how much she enjoys working in retail!

When I think back on all that has happened since you were taken from us, I must say, life has been sporadically quite hectic! We went on holiday to Morocco and although it was a struggle, it was a lovely holiday and one that I think did Megan and Regan the world of good. Do you remember the conversation that we had, when I told you it was a place I had always wanted to visit, after you had booked to go there with Meg? The trip that was booked to Italy, just after my birthday was postponed, but you'll be happy to know that it has been rescheduled for the end of this year. As a family we walked 5K in your memory, across seven of London's bridges, raising awareness for CRY. Regan moaned most of the way, so he seems to be carrying on the brotherly trait! Rich completed a half marathon and a 46 mile bike ride in your memory, we held a charity golf day and fundraising evening on what would have been your 26th birthday and all in all, so far have raised over £7500 for Cardiac Risk in the Young in your name, which is absolutely amazing.

I must say, Regan has had a few classic moments that reduced me to tears, but ones that you would have literally laughed your head off at. The first one being when we brought your ashes home and Rich went to collect Regan from school. On the way home, he was telling Regan that your ashes were home for a few days and that we had put them in your cabin. Regan pondered that thought for a few moments before delivering an astonishing request, "Dad, could I take Danny's ashes into school tomorrow, because we've got show and tell?!" Thankfully, Rich said No!! We both agreed how you would have found that hilarious! The other memorable moment was when Becky had bought me a 'Bun Bun II'. I was about to sew the pouch containing your ashes into it, when Regan asked, "Mum, what's in the blue velvet bag?" I told him that it contained some of your ashes and he asked me what they looked like. I carefully opened the bag and let him look in, I must admit to being totally unprepared for his reaction when he blurted out "Oh, it looks just like cat litter!" I was completely gobsmacked and wanted to say, "Regan, that's your brother", but I let it go and knew exactly how you would have reacted! That little brother of yours misses you terribly and spends lots of time in your room on your PS4. You are his inspiration babe; he is like you in so many ways, he's currently in the process of mastering his own variety of facial expressions and we all witness his confidence growing by the day. He's definitely his own person but is showing signs of sharing your unique sense of humour!

I admit that I often feel guilty that life has carried on for me, each day a painful reminder of what we have lost, because life is now unrecognisable to the one that we all shared with you Dan. At times, I find comfort in looking at photos of you as a baby, that cheeky red haired little boy. Those pictures bring back so many forgotten memories and make me realise what a beautiful life you had, not just as an adult but a wonderful childhood too. It makes me reflect that although your life was far too short, your life was never about the quantity of time you had, more the quality of what you did with the time you had. I believe there is only one real guarantee in life and that is, that life is not guaranteed. I spend most of my day in the past, thinking about when you were here and reminiscing things we did as a family, I like my head and heart being in the past. I've become very philosophical about the past, present and future. The present consists of just one day before it becomes the past, and as you are well aware Danny, the future holds no promises for any of us. I used to see each passing day taking you further away from me, but I've come to realise that each day is actually bringing us closer together. I bought a big memory jar and created an email address, so that friends could email me their memories of you. I have received so many lovely memories and have printed them off and placed them in the jar. I like reading them and know that Meggie and Regan will enjoy reading in the future, about some of the things you got up to with your friends, that they never knew about, any X rated ones will not be placed into the jar though sweetheart.

Looking back over the months that you have been gone, so much has happened. Your death was beyond unbelievable, not just the suddenness but everything that unravelled following it. We struggled to deal with the constant change of direction, because the more I searched for answers, the more horrendous the reality of it all became. I will never be able to come to terms with the fact that you have been denied a life, a future and a family of your own. You have been let down in the worst way imaginable darling,. Brugada syndrome is not curable, but it is treatable and sudden arrhythmic death is preventable, if only they had seen their error and sent you to a specialist when your arrhythmia was detected 8 years prior to losing you. If anyone of those GP's had done their job properly, during any one of the 18 separate visits we made to that surgery, you would still be with us today baby. I have left no stone unturned when it came to finding out why this happened to you Danny. I have uncovered failings, heard things, seen things and learned things that I wish I hadn't. You never liked loose ends baby, so I owed it to you darling to dot the 'I's and cross the T's'.
I hope that I have done you proud and I only wish that it could have made a difference.

I have struggled for so long with my own unpredictable episodes of grief, yet have lately started to accept it as it comes, rather than resist it. I see my grief as though I am sweeping up a huge pile of leaves in the garden. Some days, the leaves are all swept up into one big, neat and tidy pile, it's irregular but it's manageable, the sun shines and I can feel the warmth of it on my face. It is a nice day, a good day and although I know I'll never have another perfect day in my entire life, this is a day that I feel I can get through and maybe even enjoy. However, there are also many cloudy days, where without warning or specific reason, that once tidy pile is no more. My emotions are like those leaves, they are blown by the strongest wind of grief imaginable and instantly scattered in every different direction possible. A relentless storm of which I have no control over or idea in knowing how long it will actually last before the clouds begin clear and that whirlwind of grief will ease or finally stop. During these times, it is difficult to believe that those leaves of emotion will ever settle in a way that once again, I shall be able to collect them altogether. What I am beginning to learn though Danny, is that it will ease, the sun will break through those clouds and that storm will eventually pass. I also know that once again, I will find the strength and courage to begin to sweep my leaves of love, of loss and longing, those happy and sad memories and even that heartbreaking pain of emptiness, back into the neat and tidy pile. Yes, it will still be irregular but once again it will be manageable, until the next time. And yet regardless of how often this happens, I know I will go through the rest of my life, constantly sweeping and keeping those leaves together. Not just for my own sanity but for all of us, left here without you darling.

I will try to look forward and strive, once again to become that Mum that Steven, Becky, Megan and Regan remember. A mum who will always have their backs; always put them first and will love them unconditionally until I take my last breath. So far, I have had two tattoos done since you went away. The first one is on my forearm, it is a feather, with a dove flying towards my wrist with the quote "Your wings were ready, but my heart was not" written above and below it. The second one is an angel that I drew and have had placed between the top of my shoulder blades. It is truly beautiful Dan, the angel is a young man weeping and the tattooist has coloured the hair to match yours and also included some of your ashes into the ink when doing it. So remember when I always used to say to you that I'd have your back? Well my darling, now you will forever have mine and wherever I go, you are with me.

  We shall never stop loving you Danny and promise that you will always be part of our daily life and conversations, in exactly the same way as we did with Grandad. The spare feathers from your Day are being taken by family and friends on their holidays and will be placed in countries all over the world as they are visited and this will continue until there are no more left. Please always stay close to me, my precious boy, I see the signs you send and will never stop looking out for them. I shall never fear death, because I know you will be waiting for me, but until my time comes, I need to try the best way that I can to repair the shattered foundations of this family for Megan and Regan, Steven and Becky. Their lives need to be as amazing as yours Dan, filled with beautiful memories and happy times, just like yours. We will never stop loving or missing you Danny and we will carry the pain of losing you with us as a family, forever. Death cannot break the bond that we shared nor can it take the memories that we made together. We will continue to keep you with us always, my precious boy. You will be part of everything we do and everywhere we go forever Danny, I promise.

I love you millions, all around the world, beyond the stars, to the ends of the universe and back again.

Forever and always,
Mum xx

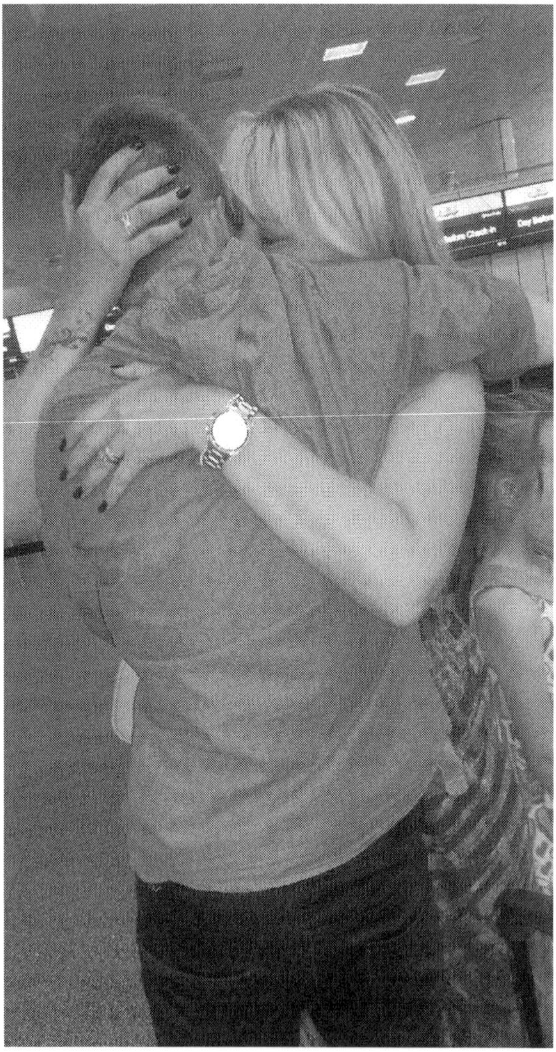

A March Winter's Wind

A March winter wind blew a soft silent breeze,
That rushed through the branches of family trees.
Unseen and unheard and to us was unknown,
As it swirled on the ground, around where ours had grown.
Despite deep entwined roots that grew strong and healthy,
That wind began to sway each bough of our tree.

With strength and a chill, the last leaves it did take,
And that March winters wind, a young branch it did break.
Drifting peacefully in the darkness, not making a sound,
The fourth highest branch softly fell to the ground.
And there it rested so gently, till the morning awoke,
Letting sunlight shine through from the place where it broke.

New leaves and blossoms, no more it shall grow,
Nor see the changing of seasons, bringing sunshine and snow.
Though that family tree, tries to heal and repair,
It forever will weep for the young branch that was there.
That beautiful tree that grew with branches of seven,
Now only bares six, because one is in heaven.

Love you forever Danny xx

"Above the darkest of clouds, the sun is shining"

CONTENTS -

DANIEL JAY
AUSTRALIA
MARCH 2017
THURSDAY 9TH MARCH
BROKEN HEARTS & HYACINTHS
DRIFTING THROUGH THE DAYS
THE CHAPEL OF REST
WEST HAM
THE MISSING BUTTERFLY
DANNY'S DAY
A HANDFUL OF ASHES
OUT OF THE BLUE
THE PSYPHIC NIGHT
SIGNS OF MY ANGEL
ST GEORGES HOSPITAL
THE MEDICAL RECORDS
A LIFE WITHOUT DAN
MEMORIES OF OTHERS
DARLING DANNY
A MARCH WINTER'S WIND

*In Loving Memory of
Daniel Jay Brown
3rd March 1992 ~ 9th March 2017*

Printed in Great Britain
by Amazon